to Lisa

It's Not You,
It's Brie

• • • • •

Unwrapping America's
Unique Culture of Cheese

Kirstin Jackson

Brie all you can Brie!

K Jackson

A Perigee Book

A PERIGEE BOOK
Published by the Penguin Group
Penguin Group (USA) Inc.
375 Hudson Street, New York, New York 10014, USA

Penguin Group (Canada), 90 Eglinton Avenue East, Suite 700, Toronto, Ontario M4P 2Y3, Canada (a division of Pearson Penguin Canada Inc.) • Penguin Books Ltd., 80 Strand, London WC2R 0RL, England • Penguin Group Ireland, 25 St. Stephen's Green, Dublin 2, Ireland (a division of Penguin Books Ltd.) • Penguin Group (Australia), 250 Camberwell Road, Camberwell, Victoria 3124, Australia (a division of Pearson Australia Group Pty. Ltd.) • Penguin Books India Pvt. Ltd., 11 Community Centre, Panchsheel Park, New Delhi—110 017, India • Penguin Group (NZ), 67 Apollo Drive, Rosedale, Auckland 0632, New Zealand (a division of Pearson New Zealand Ltd.) • Penguin Books (South Africa) (Pty.) Ltd., 24 Sturdee Avenue, Rosebank, Johannesburg 2196, South Africa

Penguin Books Ltd., Registered Offices: 80 Strand, London WC2R 0RL, England

While the author has made every effort to provide accurate telephone numbers, Internet addresses, and other contact information at the time of publication, neither the publisher nor the author assumes any responsibility for errors, or for changes that occur after publication. Further, the publisher does not have any control over and does not assume any responsibility for author or third-party websites or their content.

First edition: November 2012

Library of Congress Cataloging-in-Publication Data

Jackson, Kirstin.
It's not you, it's brie : unwrapping America's unique culture of cheese / Kirstin Jackson.
pages cm — (A Perigee book)
Includes bibliographical references and index.
ISBN 978-0-399-53766-0 (hardback)
1. Cheese—United States.   2. Cheesemaking—United States.   3. Cooking (Cheese)   I. Title.
SF274.U6J33   2012
641.6'73—dc23   2012024062

PRINTED IN THE UNITED STATES OF AMERICA

10 9 8 7 6 5 4 3 2

The recipes contained in this book are to be followed exactly as written. The publisher is not responsible for your specific health or allergy needs that may require medical supervision. The publisher is not responsible for any adverse reactions to the recipes contained in this book.

Most Perigee books are available at special quantity discounts for bulk purchases for sales promotions, premiums, fund-raising, or educational use. Special books, or book excerpts, can also be created to fit specific needs. For details, write: Special Markets, Penguin Group (USA) Inc., 375 Hudson Street, New York, New York 10014.

ALWAYS LEARNING   PEARSON

This book is dedicated to my parents, who've provided me with more support than I would have thought capable of just two people. And to artisan cheesemakers, who inspire with what they do every day: Thank you for providing such amazing cheeses to write about—I cross my fingers that you will find this book more enjoyable than cleaning milk vats at the end of the day (unless that's your thing, then bless you for your sanitary ways).

Contents

Introduction

• • • • •

American cheese has more styles than the pope has gilded robes in his Vatican armoire. There is Quesillo de Oaxaca, a Mexican-style cheese hand-stretched by the Salazars in California; Scholten Weybridge, an uber-crème made in Vermont from the milk of a rare Dutch belted cow; and Rivers Edge's Mayor of Nye Beach, a washed rind goat's milk that could knock any Époisses out of the water. None of them fit into neat categories.

Rather than boxing the abundance into eight or nine categories or trying to replicate other excellent cheese guides, this book explains American artisanal cheese according to their influences—cultural and historical backgrounds, production techniques, flavors, and uses. Here, cheeses are divided into sixteen basic genres. Then, each genre is explored by using three specific cheeses as lenses to consider that style's varied inspirations, production, and history, and to look closer at the people who are making American cheese.

I picked these specific cheeses because I think they serve as great examples of each varied category, not because I think they're necessarily better than another similar style made in the United States (although I do adore the ones I picked). In so doing, I may miss some cheese types, but I've tried to focus on the ones that have made the most impact in the United States and, by default, in my own life.

The cheeses in this book are artisanal. There are many different ways to define "artisanal" and "artisan," but in this book, an "artisanal" cheese is one that is made by craftspeople and artisans who respect the specific cheese's process and tradition, and understand their impact on it. Because this requires so much attention, most times artisanal cheese will be made by smaller cheese companies. The cheesemakers crafting "artisanal" cheeses respect their animals and their land. If the cheese is not farmstead ("farmstead" means that cheesemakers make cheese from the milk of their farm's herd), the cheesemakers respect the farmers and the animals who provide their milk as they do the cheese itself.

The recipes in this book are original and crafted to highlight the artisan cheese with which they're served. They run from appetizer to dessert, are seasonally arranged, and are inspired according to cheese style. I hope you enjoy them.

Finally, though I use the term "American" in this book for simplicity's sake, I am specifically referring to the United States of America, not the broader Americas.

A Very, Very Brief History of Cheese in the United States

There is a rhyme and reason to why certain cheese styles reign mighty in some areas versus others—why the funky scents of Limburger are banished to dairy drawers in Wisconsin fridges and don't sell much in California, and why Vermont has more creameries than Louisiana. Cheese in the United States is deeply linked to our nation's past. Like Comté in France or Pecorino in Italy, American cheese tells stories of craftsmanship, culture, and history.

For example, commodity cheddar isn't the highest-grossing wheel in the United States because of its taste alone. As Paul Kindstedt explains in his book *American Farmstead Cheese*, cheddar is the most popular cheese here because the Puritans, many of whom were from cheesemaking epicenters in Britain that focused on easily transportable, durable cheeses, brought with them their customs and spread their cheddar love at home and abroad.

Though few would dispute that the British made the biggest bang with their cheddar-style cheeses in the United States, other immigration populations such as the Dutch, Swiss, Germans, Italians, and Mexicans also influenced North American cheese with their customs.

It wasn't until the Industrial Revolution hit America that cheese became commercialized, or commoditized. Equipment became mechanized and more efficient. Women, who were the original cheesemakers in home kitchens, lost commercial control of their craft. Because large milk quantities were needed to meet higher demand and safety concerns arose with the expanding production, milk pooling became more common and pasteurization became the norm. Artisan and farmstead cheesemaking declined.

The twentieth-century drive for modernity and homogenous food marginalized the craft even more. Sure, good artisan cheese was being made here and there in small batches, but it wasn't given the time of day by most of the American public, who were happy with their modern, smooth-melting processed cheeses.

It wasn't until the 1980s that our cheese really earned back its artisan credo. As the United States prospered economically, Americans headed out to see the world. They traveled, they read books about traditional cheesemaking, and a handful of (mainly female) cheesemakers started making cheese that made people care again. Which brings us to where we are today—in a dynamic artisan cheese world. Skilled people who honor their craft, the art, and the animals and land that make it all possible are making our artisan cheeses, and they're growing in number. This gives the big processors a run for their money, and gives the rest of us wonderful things to spend our hard-earned cash on—farms, dairy, and making our stomachs happy. Long live the cornucopia of American cheese. May its bounty always outnumber the pope's gilded robes.

Prepubescent Cheese

• • • • •

The Salad Days

These young fresh cheeses are the prepubescents of the cheese world. They've matured past being just cultured cream or yogurt, have undergone acidification, have likely seen a little rennet in their lifetime, and with a drizzle of olive oil and a grind of pepper, are ready to venture out and maybe top a bruschetta or two.

But like a tween with access to their parents' Playboy channel, fresh cheeses need constant supervision. Overexposure to the world's elements can morph a young ricotta specimen from sweet and lovable to sour and bitter within twenty-four hours.

Best consumed within days or weeks after birth, the glory of fresh cheeses is linked to their immaturity. Unlike many tweens of today, fresh cheeses have a squeaky clean appearance. Most are white or a light hue, and because the milk is minimally processed, they taste like whatever the animal that provided their milk was eating that week. Once aged and tainted with the extra acidity, firmness, or rind that time deals them, most fresh cheeses loose their appeal.

The category of fresh cheeses is wide. Often anything from chèvre to mozzarella or schloss is labeled "fresh." But for this book's purposes of grouping cheeses together via similar characteristics, influences, and uses, I'm dividing up the classic "fresh" category into three families.

Here, the first "fresh" family is made up of cheeses such as chèvre, ricotta, fromage blanc, quark, Teleme, and crescenza. They are the lightest and brightest of fresh cheeses and are either best served with a bit of sea salt or olive oil to show off their simple flavors, or used in cooking. Unlike freshly made mozzarella or burrata, which become rubbery when heated, these freshies like it hot. Unpressed and unbrined, they work differently with foods than queso fresco or feta. These are the simple, handmade cheeses that have been made in kitchens, mainly by women, around the world for centuries. They require excellent milk, a deft touch, light wine and beer pairings, and constant chaperoning to make sure they stay in line.

Mystery Bay Farm Chèvre, Washington

Like taking a tattooed punk rocker to the prom after your mother set you up with the nice boy from Sunday school, making cheese can be as much a political act as a labor of love. And a much more successful and meaningful one at that.

Mystery Bay Farm in Nordland, Washington, has been making chèvre since 2008. Through their efforts to pursue their passions in farming and animal husbandry, and to show that being an independent small-time farmer is still a viable option in the current American economic system, they've created a farm and dairy that both set an example, and a cheese that demonstrates the beauty of simple things done well.

A blizzardy, school's-called-off hue of white, their chèvre—spreadable at room temperature, and crumbly when cold—is a fresh, lactic-acid-set goat cheese. Translating to "goat" in French, *chèvre* in the United States indicates a fresh, minimally processed, young goat cheese. In France, it is called *fromage blanc*.

Slightly tangy with lemony and peppery notes typical of fresh goat's milk, Mystery Bay's chèvre epitomizes the glory of the fresh milk cheeses. That is, in addition to highlighting goat's milk's basic flavors, chèvre tastes exactly like what the animals are eating. The cheese and its curds are not cooked, aged, pressed, or salted, so all you taste is milk—an expression of what lactating animals consume. In Mystery Bay you taste grass, sweet blackberries, blackberry leaves, and the occasional floral notes from western Washington's native roses, which the goats snack on during their time on the rotated pastures.

Ecologists and farmers, husband and wife owners Scott Brinton and Rachael Van Laanen chose to focus on chèvre for two main reasons. They had faith that the quality of the milk provided by their pastured animals would show marvelously in the straightforward, elegant cheese. And thanks to the goat cheese revolution of the seventies and eighties that introduced chèvre to the American masses, they also had faith in people's previous familiarity with the style, and they knew the local Port Townsend population would welcome it.

A bonus—there's no need to find cellar space or spend time flipping wheels or washing the chèvre down. It takes up little space and requires much less labor than aged cheese. To make chèvre, the milk is heated, then cooled, and cultures and rennet are added (rennet is a mix of enzymes that comes from the stomach lining of a cow, plants like thistle, or microbial molds and is responsible for coagulating and seperating curds/proteins from whey/liquid in cheesemaking). Next, the curd mass is left to sit for about twelve to fourteen hours; then it is ladled into molds, drained for twenty-four hours, salted, and packaged—all within three days. In, then out.

Which brings us to another point. Cheese is not just a passion; it can be a political product, and one that can propel families, societies, and businesses forward. There are many ways cheesemakers support and engage their community—by buying milk from local dairy farmers, by hiring community members, by being land stewards, by being small business owners. One reason why the Van Laanen–Brinton family chose to make a low-labor cheese from the milk of their small herd of goats was because by doing so, the couple could demonstrate that running an independently small, environmentally sustainable, and financially stable farm was possible in a big business–dominated world. When they sell the cheese they make with such intentions, the product takes on meaning, and the community can engage that meaning in the way of their choosing by buying the product. That, or they could just revel in the cheese's deliciousness. In Mystery Bay's case, that would likely entail cooking with the chèvre.

Its elegant simplicity, one of the things that drove Mystery Bay to the style, is also what makes chèvre such a good cooking cheese. It has a clean, pure, bright flavor that pops in any dish. As with all fresh cheeses, the more local it is, the better. Whatever chèvre you can get made from the milk of pasture-grazed animals near you will no doubt be better than one or two states away because chèvre loses its bright, lively, fresh flavor as it ages, which it inevitably does when transported long distances.

Some other favorite chèvres besides Mystery Bay are those from Harley Farms from Pescadero, California; Prodigal Farm from Rougemont, North Carolina; Dancing Goat from Byron Center, Michigan; and Catapano from Long Island, New York.

Salvatore Bklyn Ricotta, New York

If you thought ricotta was just a lasagna filler killing space between the noodles and sauce until the real dairy prize—the hot, buttery, oozing, white mozzarella—arrived, Salvatore Bklyn Ricotta will prove you wrong. This ricotta is a wolf in sheep's clothing.

At first glance, one might confuse Salvatore with the everyday grainy, low-flavor, nondescript cheese of the same name sold at chain supermarkets. But a second look reveals a ricotta story of flavor, complexity, and Italian culture. That, and it shows why Italian grandmothers devote canolli space to ricottas when there's perfectly good pastry cream nearby.

The color of cream spooned from the top of a milk bottle, Salvatore is at once fluffier, thicker, and richer than its supermarket cousins. Its flavor is a mix of sweet floral milk and rich, salted butter with a light crème fraîche tang. It begs to be spread over freshly baked, crusty bread, drizzled with olive oil, and then left alone with the other guys so it can show what it's made of.

↣ Salvatore Bklyn Ricotta

Despite its prowess, according to some purist cheese folk, Salvatore ricotta is not real ricotta. "True" ricotta is an ingenious value-added cheesemaking by-product. In Italy, cheesemakers discovered that if they heated the liquid (whey) that remained after the milk proteins/solids firmed and coagulated, and maybe added a tad more milk, even more cheesy protein would gather and give them two cheeses for the price of one. Little to no fresh milk or cream is added. This type of ricotta tastes less rich, and is very, very authentic. (It can be spotted driving fast cars, doesn't take milk in its coffee after noon, and wears a shirt that says, "I Am Authentic Italian; Just Ask Me.")

Although most wouldn't kick Salvatore off bruschetta, most Italians and many proud Italian-Americans would not consider it ricotta. If an Italian grandmother made anything similar to it in her home, she'd probably call it "home cheese."

But since part of the charm of American cheesemaking is its willingness to be playful and take risks with traditional archetypes, and Salvatore tastes more representative of excellent Italian ricotta than most "true" mass-produced versions out there, let's close our formaggio dictionary for a moment and roll with it.

Betsy Devine started making Salvatore as a chef in Brooklyn's Lunetta restaurant kitchen because she wasn't happy with what was on the market. She wanted more than just something to stuff between noodles; she wanted a cheese that made her customers revel in the notion of ricotta. Devine quickly developed a following of chefs, and later, cheese shops, that were smitten with her cheese.

Inspired by a trip to Italy, where Devine and her wife and business partner, Rachel Mark, met a charismatic ricotta genius named Salvatore, Devine left the restaurant biz and the two opened a ricotta company.

Salvatore uses a combination of mainly milk and some cream from Hudson Valley Fresh, a small cooperative of family-run farms in

Upstate New York. Devine heats the blend and adds lemon juice to encourage the curds and whey to separate. Once the curds emerge, they're gently scooped into a perforated plastic tub lined with cheesecloth so the liquid can drain from the creamy curds overnight and become a thick, rich cheese that spreads in small, rich grains.

With its fresh, sweet, milky flavors, ricotta is a cheese that's typically employed to bring a balanced richness to dishes, in lasagna, as a pasta filling, and in traditional Italian desserts. Yet a good ricotta really shows its stuff served in plainest form. Salvatore made its name at the Brooklyn Flea Market, for example, spooned over toasted bruschetta and drizzled with olive oil. To show off ricotta's simple flavors, serve with a lean wine, such as a sparkling Prosecco or Cava, Sauvignon Blanc or Grechetto. Other creameries' ricottas to try are Bellwether Creamery from Sonoma, Calfornia (they make a ricotta from cow's and sheep's milk whey, as well as a fresh, whole cow's milk ricotta, available mainly in California); Alleva Dairy from New York, New York (made from cow's milk whey, available in New York); Jacobs Creamery from Chehalis, Washington (whole cow's milk ricotta, found around the Pacific Northwest); and Catapano Dairy from Peconic, New York (whole goat's milk, available in New York and by mail order).

Franklin's Teleme, California

Franklin's Teleme gets you with its innocent puppy dog eyes. Sitting low to the cheese board in its quiet rectangular shape with little adornment, rind, or color to speak of, the humble cheese suggests its only need in life is to be eaten—fresh or cooked, as long as it's with love.

After one bite, that's all you want for the Teleme, too. Well, that and to have its sweet, subtle creaminess waiting for you over polenta with a glass of Trebbiano in hand when you get home from work every night.

Teleme is most closely related to crescenza in the Italian *stracchino* family of cheeses, but it didn't start out that way.

According to Teleme cheesemaker Franklin Peluso, the first batch of Teleme was made by a man trying to make Turkish feta-like cheese, otherwise known as *telemes*. The *telemes* attempt was a bust, but the outcome was a hit. The resulting sweet, subtle, creamy, mild cheese stood about an inch high, turned into a puddle of cream when melted, and tasted just like crescenza.

The original stracchinos, off-white, creamy Northern Italian cheeses meant to be consumed quickly, were made with milk from *stracca* (tired) cows. Hiking around the Lombardy hills took its toll on the cows, and at the end of the day, their milk was higher in fat (less water content) and more acidic. These high-moisture, rich yet subtle cheeses with lemony flavors were staples of the region—served for dessert, over foccacia, or used in cooking.

With a large Italian immigrant population craving stracchino, cities such as San Francisco were an easy market for Teleme back in the twenties. The West Coast Italian-American Pelusos started crafting their own version with a lightly coated rice flour rind and joined the two other Teleme forces in San Francisco in filling North Beach deli cases.

Yet despite an increase in the cheese's sales when Italian imports were restricted during World War II and a spike in popularity in the sixties, Teleme fell out of fashion toward the end of the century. The Pelusos looked to other cheese styles to stay afloat and the other two Teleme producers went under. When Franklin Peluso's father taught him how to make the cheeses in the 1980s, Teleme sales were at an all-time low, and in 2005, the Pelusos sold their company. Franklin, however, kept his vision and his cheesecloth handy and opened his own company.

Now, Peluso focuses entirely on making the cheese that stole his heart the first time he hand-shaped the curds (word around town is that he might also release a washed rind version). For him, Teleme is a source of family pride and responsibility. Because of its high moisture content and tart bite, it's a fussy cheese. Few knew how to make it right, and most of those who did have either retired or died. And, Peluso says, he's not sharing the recipe.

Regardless of whether cheesemakers will only be inducted into the Teleme club after swearing (blindfolded, with all three hands tied behind their back) never to reveal its secrets, the cheese has touched many. Every time Peluso makes Teleme, he feels a sense of duty toward those who have told him that his cheese makes them smile because it tastes like their childhood fifty years ago. So Peluso continues to hand-press every batch.

Because Franklin's Teleme has a rice flour rind that absorbs moisture, it lasts longer than the classic crescenza-stracchino. Unlike other soft stracchino relatives that have a week or two shelf life before they start to taste sour or bitter, Teleme gains power and gets gooier as it ages. Franklin's version most closely resembles the original when young and can be eaten until you can no longer take the accumulating strength (i.e., funk).

Traditionally stracchino cheeses are primarily used in cooking, to top risotto, crostini, or for dessert with fresh fruit and honey. They are also a good light starter served at room temperature, or baked, and drizzled with olive oil and cracked pepper. Eat with straightforward wines as with other prepubescent freshies—Grechettos, Trebbianos, unoaked Chardonnays, Southwestern French blends, and stick to the lightest beers possible, like a Pilsner. Franklin's Teleme is available at select stores around the country, but if you can't find it near you, try another local, crescenza-stracchino style, such as Bellwether crescenza from Sonoma, California, or Mozzarella Company's from Dallas, Texas. However, expect a much shorter shelf life—the original crescenza styles can turn as quickly as a fresh ricotta.

Herbed-Polenta Teleme Squares

These seared polenta squares serve as a gentle base for the mild Teleme cheese, and the Teleme serves as a base for a seasonal topping of your preference. I like asparagus tips, heirloom tomatoes, figs, or persimmons in the height of their season, or just eating the squares plain when I'm in the mood for serious comfort food. The squares can be served as hors d'oeuvres, or if topped heavily and cut in larger pieces, as improvised pizza bases as part of a main course. Many young, mild, soft cheeses such as chèvre or fromage blanc (drain in a sieve if very wet) or fresh ricotta could be used as substitutes.

> 1 cup polenta
> 3½ cups water
> 1 teaspoon salt
> 1 small ancho chile
> 1 bay leaf
> ⅛ cup parsley, chopped
> 1 teaspoon rosemary, finely chopped
> 1–2 tablespoons butter
> salt and pepper to taste
> ⅓–½ pound Teleme

Put the polenta, water, and salt in a medium-sized, heavy-bottomed pot. Whisk together well to mix. Bring the mixture to a boil while whisking occasionally to blend and to ensure the polenta on the bottom of the pot doesn't burn. Once the polenta has come to a boil, add the chile and bay leaf and turn the heat as low as possible, making sure you still see small bubbles. Continue stirring occasionally and scraping the bottom of the pan (switch from a whisk to a wooden spoon as the polenta thickens for easier stirring) for 15–20 minutes. You want a soft polenta with its small kernels still a little firm. Stir in the herbs and, if needed, add salt and pepper to taste.

Spread the polenta on a cookie sheet covered with buttered parchment paper or a silicone mat. Use a cake spatula to make smooth. Let cool. Cut into small, easy-to-pick-up squares.

WHEN READY TO SERVE:

Preheat the broiler.

Bring a medium-sized sauté pan to medium-high heat and add a half-tablespoon of butter. Working in batches, sear the polenta squares until their edges are crispy, and set aside on a cookie sheet. Once done with all the polenta, cut pieces of Teleme just smaller than the squares and place one on each rectangle. Broil the squares on the cookie sheet until the Teleme starts to bubble and become golden. Add your desired toppings to the squares and serve.

Pasta Filata

• • • • •

Young, Soft, and Flexible

If the former fresh category of cheeses was tween-style, then this second fresh category is full-on teen. Ear piercing, bringing dates home, staying out past ten o'clock on a weekend, teen. Pasta filata cheeses make up the second category of fresh cheeses in this book, and they have seen more than just a little acidification and rennet in their day. They've been spun around the cheese block.

Pasta filata roughly translates to "spun curds." A style that originated in Italy, pasta filata cheeses are normally as white (if not whiter) as their tween siblings, clean, buttery, milky-tasting, soft, and plush. Common fresh styles are mozzarella, burrata, and Quesillo de Oaxaca. There are some aged cheeses of this style, such as provolone, that are made in similar fashion, but because their presence in the United States isn't as prevalent or artisanal, we'll narrow our discussion of pasta filata to the fresh versions.

First comes the Southern Italian archetype, mozzarella. Then, variations of that form. The category is called spun curd because, unlike most other cheeses, the curds are stretched or, especially in the case of Quesillo de Oaxaca, spun. Warm water or whey is poured over the curds to make them pliable. Once they're pliable, the curds are stretched anywhere up to twenty or so feet, depending on the cheese type. Like people in a yoga class, the cheese becomes elastic when stretched.

Pasta filata's presence was documented as early as the fourteenth century in Italy and made its way to the United States when a large number of Italians emigrated to the country in the nineteenth and twentieth centuries. It's been suggested that the pasta filata technique was later translated via Italian monks to Mexico during periods of colonization, and according to Moises Salazar, a cheesemaker at Queso Salazar whose family's cheese will be profiled in this chapter, Quesillo de Oaxaca was invented at the turn of the twentieth century in Oaxaca.

Though Quesillo de Oaxaca is celebrated for its superior melting ability (I would have had a heck of a time playing with this cheese as a child if I'd known about its legendary threading), artisanal mozzarella and burrata are revered for their plush, moist texture. Such high-moisture cheeses don't normally melt like the rubbery white balls labeled "low fat" sold in grocery stores. They will spread when heated, but most high-moisture pasta filata cheeses aren't known for their threading or warmed stringability—except Quesillo. They melt well enough in lasagna, though, and are delicious on sandwiches, or plain and drizzled with a little olive oil.

Fresh pasta filata cheeses can be a little fussy like the ricottas in the previous fresh family. Burrata is best consumed within a week after production. Fresh mozzarella can last longer because it is lower in moisture than the cream-filled burrata, but its flavor is best closest to production, too. Like the drier pasta filata provolone, Quesillo de Oaxaca can last from weeks to months, but it also tastes best when freshest. All pasta filata cheeses are best with simple wines, or paired to alcohol according to the dish in which they're cooked.

Lioni Latticini Mozzarella, New Jersey

Mozzarella is a serious thing in a family of fifth-generation cheese-makers from Campania, Italy. Just ask Sal (Giuseppe) Salzarulo, co-owner of Lioni Latticini Inc.

Mozzarella as wonderful as Lioni's wasn't always in America, much less New Jersey. Salzarulo was running his importing company that brought in dried pastas from Italy when he first tasted a batch of the pasta filata cheese at a shop where he sold his wares. It was less than fantastic. He asked the owner why he sold subpar mozzarella. When the miffed shop owner asked him if he could do better, Salzarulo said he could, and he made up some very impressive batches in his garage that set the foundation for the Lioni business.

Soon thereafter, Salzarulo left his pasta-importing business to spread the pasta filata love with his nephew and Lioni co-owner, Salvatore Salzarulo. Spreading the love is no stretch (pardon the pasta filata pun). The family is very generous with their knowledge—during our interview, Sal kept telling me how to make great mozzarella at home when all I really wanted to know was how they made their gems at Lioni.

My favorite Lioni mozzarella size, the Ovoline, is an egg-shaped mozzarella ball that comes packed in eight-ounce retail cups or three-pound containers and fits happily nestled in one's palm. It's as white as whipped cream and comes in a variety of ways, from hand-wrapped to water-packed. It's smooth, moist, delicate, and tastes like fresh cream. The pure taste reveals that the company never skimps on using extremely fresh, high-quality milk in its immaculately clean plants.

When Lioni started, Sal Salzarulo made it all by hand in his garage. Now Lioni is made in two stages in two different factories. First, the curds are made in a plant in Upstate New York.

Pasteurized whole milk from Upstate New York is inoculated with cultures, then rennet. Once the curd has settled, about twenty-five to thirty minutes later, and looks like jelly, it's cut into popcorn-sized pieces. Then the curds and whey are stirred to firm the curd, the curd is allowed to settle again, and the whey is drained. Next the curd is cooled, bundled up, vacuum-packed, and loaded on a truck to go to New Jersey that night.

The New Jersey factory begins production at 5 a.m. the next morning in preparation for mozzarella. This is the when the curd becomes pasta filata in the Salzarulo family's custom-engineered Italian curd-stretching machine. The curd is warmed up with a little hot water in a stainless steel vat to loosen it up a bit, but only with a small amount of water because the curd loses butterfat if left to sit, says Sal. Then, it is pushed to the front of another tank, where two metal claws stretch the curd just as one would with their fingers at home. Next the soft, stretched curd is pushed to the front of the machine and through a little set of doors to the molding area. This machine molds the mozzarella into the appropriate size, from the one-gram Perline to a sixteen-ounce ball.

The thing to remember with fresh mozzarella (not those "mozzarella" blocks grated over chain restaurant pizzas) is that it's best eaten shortly after made. Mozzarella such as Lioni lasts longer than burrata, but it still has a short life span in comparison with aged cheeses. I like it best in the first or second week.

This mozzarella is best on its own with a Prosecco or lightly creamy tasting, unoaked Italian white wine such as Tocai Friulano. I'm not a big fan of it with beer—it quickly overwhelms the fresh cheese. If you're cooking with mozzarella (the high-moisture ovoline just melts a little, but Lioni also makes a lower-moisture variety that forms stretchy threads), pair the wine to whatever dish you're cooking. Barbera with lasagna, for example, or Viognier when topping a butternut squash soup.

Lioni Latticini's mozzarella can be found all over the East Coast, in many states nationwide, and via mail order (check online for store locations and ordering information). Lioni has a unique style, but I encourage you to taste other mozzarellas when given the chance.

Gioia Burrata, California

As a child, you quickly learn that there are good and bad times to ask your parents for something. When Dad's late for a dinner that Mom cooked after a ten-hour workday—that's a bad time. After Mom just gets a raise and comes home to find Dad folding clean laundry—that's a superb time.

As a cheese writer, if I ever had to ask coagulated milk for a favor, I'd do it right after it becomes burrata. Not only does it start out with the knowledge that it's going to be adored after it's made, but its curds have just sat in a hot water bath then been stretched out, massaged, surrounded with cream, and wrapped in a warm mozzarella blanket. Burrata is mozzarella after the most luscious of spa days.

Gioia burrata is one of the happiest burratas of the lot. It is the epitome of fresh cheese. Although it doesn't look like much packed to the brim in its white plastic, one-pound tub with its modest Gioia red, white, and green logo, once it is spooned onto a plate, Gioia reveals its delicate vigor.

After its thin outer layer is sliced open, the creamy, curd-filled interior spills out, and you're done for. Trying to set down a spoon when Gioia's sweet flavors and rich, fluffy innards are in front of you is as easy as eating just one tiny candy bar at Halloween.

Made in El Monte, Los Angeles County, California, by Vito Girardi, who is often credited with introducing burrata to the United States in the nineties, Gioia burrata (like all burrata) starts off the same way as mozzarella. Mozzarella curds are produced as if they were going to become the real thing—with the same amount of milk, rennet cultures, etc. Then after the curds are formed, the burrata action starts. Half the curds are stretched as if they were going to be mozzarella, and the other half are prepared for the filling.

The filling curds are shredded by hand into tiny pieces, then mixed with whole cream and set aside. Then, the other half is stretched, two pieces at a time, into small, completely smooth ("No chunks allowed," says Girardi) balls. This is the tough part. When forming the balls, the cheesemakers must work with curds so hot that, even when wearing gloves, they might need to dip their fingers in cool water for a quick respite. After the balls are formed, they're flattened and the creamy curds are nestled inside the thin mozzarella sheath and closed into a sphere. In Italy, a top knot is made with the shell that forms into a harder cheese piece, but Girardi skips this step, seeing it just as a waste of time. "I'd rather just close the ball, I already make mozzarella."

Girardi learned how to make burrata (and mozzarella, and ricotta, and scarmoza, for that matter) from his family in Pulgia, Italy, the region from which burrata comes. He says his father dragged him into the business when he was very young so "I wasn't playing in the street," and except for a brief intermission for army service, he's been working with fresh cheese since he was fourteen.

The key to enjoying burrata, says Girardi, is enjoying it fresh. Although he's opened a pack of Gioia more than twelve days after it was made and the cheese was passable, he thinks it should be eaten within five days of production. This is because burrata is so high in moisture that it can go bad very quickly. Burrata was even experiencing a popularity decline in Italy for a while, explained Girardi, because transportation issues led to unhappy customers getting their cheese too late, and thus spoiled. Trying to find perfectly fresh burrata can be almost as thrilling as eating it.

Keep in mind those pure, clean flavors when pairing with alcohol. They don't like to be disturbed. Think light and fresh. For wines, go as simple as possible—Sauvignon Blancs, Proseccos and Cavas, Vermentinos, Verdicchios and Melon de Bourgognes from the Muscadet region of France. No red wines, unless you want to taste just red wine (if that's the case, a swig from the bottle works just as well), and no oak ever. Don't even think about it. *Do*, however, think about introducing sake into the equation. A subtle, slightly floral *junmai daigingo* with a creamy finish would complement burrata's freshness. A light session or saison beer might fit here, but stay away from anything that looks darker than a banana peel.

Serve burrata with little adornment. I like it best with sea salt and olive oil over crostini. If you're serving it with a salad or as an appetizer, keep the cheese itself simple and only dress up the lettuce or sides with which it's served. Or serve as Girardi likes best, solo.

Although Gioia makes other pasta filata–style and fresh cheeses, their claim to fame is their burrata. It can be purchased via their website, and must be shipped overnight. Some other good stateside burratas to try if Gioia isn't near you or if you want to further explore are Bel Fiore from Berkeley, California; Maplebrook Farms from Bennington, Vermont; and Lioni from Union, New Jersey.

Queso Salazar Quesillo de Oaxaca, California

If you've always believed that string cheese's true home was in lunchboxes, next to carrot nubs and peanut butter and jelly sandwiches, prepare to have Queso Salazar's Oaxacan-style artisan string cheese alter your cheese mind. Alternatively, if you've been eating your child's snacks when no one's looking because you thought your pas-

Queso Salazar Quesillo de Oaxaca

sion for stringy cheese was unsophisticated, let go of your shame. Your passion is well founded.

Made in Brentwood, California, Queso Salazar's Quesillo de Oaxaca is a cheese traditional to the Oaxaca region of Mexico that pulls apart in long, string-like pieces and melts in threads longer than the Golden Gate Bridge. A traditional quesillo, Queso Salazar's cheese is a ball that's formed by wrapping a thin, five- to twenty-foot strip of stretched cheese curd around itself until it forms a sphere that looks like a much prettier, less colorful version of a rubberband ball.

Its color ranges from pure white to lightly butter colored and it tastes like clean, creamy, buttery, salty milk. When fresh from the stretching table, quesillo is supple and fluffy and just a little firmer than fresh mozzarella. After it hits the refrigerator, it solidifies slightly until it has a semifirm consistency like Monterey Jack.

The Salazar's Quesillo de Oaxaca is made nearly the same way that wife and husband seventy-year-old Estela and eighty-year-old Moises Salazar used to make it together in Oaxaca. The two still make the cheese together, along with their children (who convinced their parents to join them in Calfornia nine years after they moved there in 1995) and sometimes their grandchildren, such as Emily, a burgeoning cheesemaker in the family. And by making cheese "along with" their children, I mean sometimes all at once.

At any one time, anyone from the eighty-year-old grandfather patriarch, who very slowly walks from the stretching table to the vat to check the curd, to the only one of their nine children who doesn't like milk can be found making quesillo. Watching them make quesillo together is like watching a finely tuned orchestra play a piece they've had mastered for years. You get the feeling that any Salazar (or their newest employee, Lupe, who is fondly teased by the sisters in the family) could switch stations with another and still pull off one of the best quesillos north of Mexico.

Daughter of Estela and Moises, Amelia Salazar and her husband, Rico Millan, generally get the quesillo party started. They first pasteurize whole milk they buy from a local, pasture-based family farm in nearby Escalon. Then they add the cultures and rennet. The curd generally takes from one to two hours to set. According to Amelia, who shakes her head while smiling about the original recipe, if they started with raw milk as is traditional in Oaxaca, they wouldn't need to add cultures or wait as long for the curd to set. Because the cheese is aged under sixty days here, however, in go the cultures (letting the cheese age beyond sixty days would morph the quesillo into a totally different product).

The grandparents arrive at the Queso Salazar every Wednesday (quesillo day) to stretch the cheese. When they arrive, the quesillo stations are already set up. A pot of hot, salted water is simmering on a portable flame and three plastic tubs are arranged on milk crates so they're about waist level across from each other in a triangle pattern.

First, they scoop curds that have been sitting in the vat since they were first cut after coagulation to the first tub, where someone starts breaking up the curd into tiny pieces with their fingers. They then pass the tub to the next person and start the process again. The next person in the line pours a saucepan's worth of hot water over the crushed curds to warm them. Then, with the back of a huge wooden spoon from Oaxaca whose bowl looks like half of a coconut shell, they push and massage the curds until they become one unified, silky mass. The three people alternate between steps one and two, passing the tubs along as necessary. Once the curd is one soft piece, they shape it by picking up a curd section and running their hands gently down the curd to form one long strand that looks like an inch-wide taffy snake. All must be done very quickly or the curd will become too hard.

The strand is then handed over to others waiting an arm's distance away at a stainless steel table. Depending on the ball size, they stretch the curd from five to twenty-five feet, and then salt it. Then, the stretched piece of cheese is wrapped around itself to make the famed quesillo ball. In cheese shops, Quesillo de Oaxaca comes in smaller balls one pound and under. At most Mexican or Latino markets, quesillo is cut to order by unrolling a five-pound or so ball until the customer gets their desired length. Quesillo balls are generally one pound or larger, but occasionally make their way to the lucky hands of a Queso Salazar visitor grape-sized, wrapped by deft eighty-year-old hands to look like tiny roses.

As with all artisan cheeses, let Queso Salazar come to room temperature before serving. It will gain back some of the plush elasticity it loses through refrigeration (the Salazars almost never refrigerate their personal quesillo, preferring it the same consistency it is fresh from the table). It's fantastic eaten on its own; melted in quesadillas, in enchiladas, and on pizzas; or paired to wine or beer according to what it's melted with, or served with mescal—the Oaxacan version of tequila.

If Queso Salazar isn't available near you—Salazar is generally found just in the San Francisco Bay Area, but they might ship if you ask them nicely—try another local production Quesillo de Oaxaca near you. Another I've enjoyed is that from Cesar's Cheese in Columbus, Wisconsin, which is more widely available across the country, and I've heard fabulous things about Licon Dairy's version (called asadero) in El Paso, Texas, which is only available in Texas.

Watermelon and Burrata Salad
with Pomegranate Molasses Vinaigrette

MAKES 5–6 SERVINGS

There's no denying the delectability of the classic watermelon ricotta salad. But this one is better, as Gioia burrata offers a creamy tang to the melon that a hard, salted cheese cannot, and the oil-cured black olives give the burrata and watermelon the salt they need to bring them into the savory side while simultaneously bringing out their sweetness. When drizzled lightly over the composed yet rustic salad, the mint, basil, and pomegranate in the vinaigrette offer a just-bold-enough bite to the dish to make it pop.

• Vinaigrette •

20 oil-cured black olives, pitted and chopped fine
4 tablespoons extra virgin olive oil
2 tablespoons pomegranate molasses
9 mint leaves, finely chopped
6 basil leaves, finely chopped
½ teaspoon salt

• Salad •

2 pounds seedless watermelon
10 ounces Gioia burrata at room temperature
12 oil-cured black olives, pitted
4 mint leaves, chiffonaded
4 basil leaves, chiffonaded
freshly ground pepper to taste

Mix the chopped olives, olive oil, molasses, and chopped mint and basil together in a small bowl. Set aside.

Trim and cut the watermelon by removing its rind and slicing the fruit into cubes varying from ½ inch to an inch. Divide the watermelon evenly on five to six salad plates.

Lightly pull apart the burrata, and distribute over the watermelon, being careful to give each plate equal parts of the burrata creamy's center and firm exterior. Sprinkle the pitted olives, mint, and basil chiffonades over the salad.

Lightly spoon the vinaigrette over the salad. Add freshly ground pepper to taste.

NOTE: The pomegranate molasses can found in the international section of the supermarket or in Arabic markets, but if unavailable near you, make a balsamic reduction by cooking down the vinegar at a low heat by 50 percent and using this as a replacement.

If you use another burrata besides Gioia, which is not packed in water, weigh only the cheese itself and not any brine it comes in when determining how much to use for the recipe.

The Crumbly

• • • • •

Cheeses in Pieces

"Cheeses in Pieces" is a broad category, for nearly every dairy-eating culture has a cheese meant to cube or crumble. From feta to queso frescos like panela to paneer, these lightly fermented and slightly aged cheeses are used both fresh and in cooking—probably in as many ways as a Bedazzler was used on denim in the eighties. Not wanting to leave such an essential part of their food culture behind, immigrants from all over—from Europe to India—brought the recipes for these kitchen staples with them and made them at home, and as demand grew, some went pro. They have quickly become a part of our cheese culture.

Most of the Cheeses in Pieces are minimally processed, in that while their curds have likely seen rennet, they haven't been stretched or pulled, and most haven't been aged more than sixty days. They are light in color and have no rind. With several exceptions, these staples are relatively easy to make at home with the right inspiration.

Some of the cheeses in this category, such as queso blanco or panela, are very fresh. These cheeses are meant to add a fresh, milky flavor to dishes and are generally crumbled on foods (on top of tacos, for example) after cooking and not used during the cooking process. Paneer, a semifirm, cubed, unsalted, very fresh cheese is an exception and often used in cooked dishes such as saag paneer.

Then there are the brined crumbly cheeses such as feta. Originally from Greece but now an important food in many parts of Eastern Europe and the Middle East, feta is used in cooked and fresh dishes such as the famed Greek tomato-cucumber salad. These cheeses are stored in a saltwater brine (often whey-based) that at feta's inception was intended to preserve the cheese in warm climates. This brine can ripen the cheese as it sits.

A few Cheeses in Pieces have more age to them, such as some queso secos and añejos. Translating to dry or aged cheeses, this category envelopes an amazing variety of cheeses in Latin America, most of which have not made it yet to the United States. Out of the few prominent ones that have, cotija is a good example of a crumbly that's meant to last. These drier cheeses are used to give greater depth to cooked dishes and, like with feta, with the intention of adding a little salt in dairy form.

Cheese in Pieces is more than just fun to say. This family is fun to experiment with in fresh and cooked forms. So put away that Bedazzler and embrace this even better way to liven up one's life, dairy style.

Narragansett Queso Blanco, Rhode Island

If you ask most North Americans to name a Latin American cheese, they'll probably think of the soft, fluffy white cheese that tops their taqueria fare and say *"queso fresco."* It's true, that is queso fresco. However, there are so many types of fresh cheeses south of the North American border that calling something queso fresco is like just calling Stephen Colbert a comedian—there's so much more beyond the initial label.

Queso fresco comes in many shapes and forms in South America and can taste as different from country to region as coffee from neighboring cafés. Queso blanco, panela, and requesón all fall into the queso fresco genre, and though the wide range of frescos may not show up in many of our artisan cheese shops or grocery stores, they're alive and kicking.

Often queso frescos are just labeled as such rather than panela or requesón to cater to a sense of familiarity in consumers not intimate with Latin-style cheeses. Other times, North Americans just call white, soft or semisoft, crumbly, Latin Amerian–style cheeses *fresco* out of habit. Hopefully books about Mexican cheese, such as those written by cheese writer and consultant Carlos Yescas, will offer more education for the Latin American cheese novice (myself included).

In a market dominated by large North American companies, Narragansett Creamery in Rhode Island makes a killer queso blanco—a queso fresco–style cheese made without herbs or spices in the Guatemalan style. An inch high and the width of an ice cream quart, this queso blanco is a soft, muted white. It is a little crumblier than similar cheeses made outside Guatemala and becomes more granular and powdery instead of chunky when crumbled into pieces.

This queso blanco is a very subtle cheese. Its intention is not to add a lively saltiness to dishes as with some queso secos; it is to offer a pure expression of sweet milkiness. Eating it is like taking a swig of sweet, fresh milk from a local farm that's been topped with unsalted, cultured, melted butter.

Narragansett Creamery cofounder Louella Hill, the cofounding Frederico family, and Narragansett cheesemaker, Arturo Mendez, do everything in their power to preserve the sweet fresh flavor of the milk they use because that's what makes the cheese so awesome. The Rhode Islanders didn't actually plan on making queso blanco when they first got started, but when Mendez's small queso blanco batches created a huge demand in the local Guatemalan community, the company happily added the cheese to their repertoire.

To make the queso blanco the way that Mendez made it as a cheesemaker in Guatemala, Narragansett starts out by warming milk they purchased from neighboring small New England farms. They add a very small amount of cultures, says cofounder Hill, so the milk doesn't develop much acid and the lactose sugars stay sweet. Then they add vegetarian rennet, thirty minutes later cut the curd with a curd harp (a contraption with metal strings) to one-inch pieces, and "gently churn the curds so they don't tighten up and lose moisture like Asiago or cheddar," says Hill.

After a quick churn, the curds are allowed to settle before whey is poured off. Then the curds are gathered and salted gradually to highlight flavors, to slowly dry the curd, and to stop acid development (i.e. increase sweetness in this case). Next the curds are hand milled, says Hill, "so you're using your hands to both squeeze the curds and as paddles" until the large curds turn to the size of rice. Then all is hand packed into molds and set aside. Three to four days later the cheese is ready.

Hill likes the cheese best at its freshest, as early as four days after it's made, but admits it tastes good up to four weeks later. One way (the best way, in Hill's opinion) to serve the queso blanco is in a typical Guatemalan breakfast—served atop sunny-side-up eggs on a corn tortilla crisped over an open flame or with honey on fresh bread. When pairing queso fresco to beverages, pair according to the dish in which it's served. Queso fresco is tasty on its own, but it's an even better cooking and finishing cheese.

Several other queso frescos I've enjoyed are Mozzarella Company's queso blanco from Dallas, Texas; and Shepherd's Way Shepherd's Hope (described as a queso fresco style, but made with sheep's milk in Nerstrand, Minnesota). Try whatever's near you.

Ardith Mae Feta, Pennsylvania

Ardith Mae's cheesemaker Shereen Wilcox quietly laughs, "It's a little embarrassing that you're asking me how I make my feta for your book, because it's so easy. It's hard to make a bad batch!"

Wilcox makes more than six different cheeses. All are more cultured, complex, aged, and difficult to craft than her feta—which might explain why getting attention for something so simple to make

Feta

seems almost like undeserved praise. But it still doesn't explain how or why her brined goat's milk cheese is so darned good.

A brick as white as yogurt and as bouncy as rare steak, Ardith Mae feta is a plush brined cheese experience. Not quite as aged as many on the market, this goat's milk cheese has a little extra cushion. It crumbles in fluffy, rich pieces. It tastes lush, too. Sweet like the milk from which it comes, and nuanced with floral and lemon highlights, this feta's flavors and fluffy texture make it stand out in a sea of bobbing white bricks in salty feta brine.

Who knew feta had it in it?

Well, Wilcox did. Half-Iranian, Wilcox grew up with feta on her table every day, and despite its low yield in the cheese room, she insisted that she had to have it in her life. "I couldn't imagine *not* making it," she said.

Reportedly originally from the Middle East, feta's reign spans from the Middle East to the Mediterranean. Traditionally made from sheep's or sheep and goat's milk blends (sheep and goats thrived on many of the regions' rocky mountains), feta is a "brined cheese," as in, it sits and ages in a brine made up of water, salt, and its own whey.

To make her staple, Wilcox starts off with hot pasteurized milk, to which she adds a farmhouse culture and rennet. Then she lets the rennet settle for about an hour and cuts the curd. The curds then settle again for about fifteen minutes. After the rest, Wilcox ladles them into large, rectangular perforated stainless steel molds lined with cheesecloth. She flips the curds a couple times within three or four hours to make sure they drain evenly, and later that evening, she cuts the curd into bricks and salts them. The next day they're brined in a low-salt solution and sold within two days to about two weeks.

The make is simple enough. Ardith Mae's aging is a little different than others in that it's not brined in very salty water and is sold a lot fresher (equals creamier, less aged) than many others, but the main differences between fetas from small guys such as Ardith Mae's and the big guys is how the milk integrity affects the final product.

Because Ardith Mae is a farmstead creamery, the milk doesn't have to travel, the milk structure stays intact, and the flavors stay sweeter. With a cheese as simple as feta, it's the little things that matter. Plus, the farther a milk such as goat or sheep has to travel, the less fresh (clean) it's going to taste.

They also handle only a very small herd—fifty or so—which makes it easier to ensure the animals stay healthy and groomed. ("Once you get over fifty animals," Wilcox says, "it's hard to trim all those little hooves.") Shereen and her husband, Ardith Mae co-owner Todd Wilcox, spend a lot of time thinking about their goats.

They chose their specific property because it was in an area that they knew their animals would love, in the rockiest mountain area of Pennsylvania. Directly behind the house is a steep hillside, and as demonstrated in Greece, the Pyrenees, and the Wilcoxes' backyard, goats love to put their legendary surefooted reputation to the test. They can climb almost vertically. And as Wilcox points out, deep-rooted plants that grow on the rocky hills surrounding their property pull minerals up from the soil and make the perfect goat snacking material. It's known far and wide that goats like to browse and climb, but it's rare they have such a playground.

When Wilcox enjoys the feta from her prized goats, she often eats it the way she did when she was a child, with tomato, onions, cucumbers, and mayo on pita. Now she eats it with pasta, in lasagna, and in watermelon salads.

One of my favorite ways to eat feta is baked. Pop a half-inch slice in the oven heated to 375 degrees for about ten minutes, and you'll have a crispy, warm cheese that stays a little crumbly when set atop bread. Drizzle with olive oil. If having plain, serve with a light white such as Sauvignon Blanc, sparkling, or Verdejo from Spain. If you'd like to add it to heavier dishes, pair according to the dish's flavor or sauce.

Wilcox's feta is a seasonal item, and mainly available only in Pennsylvania and around Manhattan (Lucy's Whey in the Chelsea Market was nice enough to rush-mail me some), so be prepared to look elsewhere. But there are many other gems to be found. Other great fetas include but are not limited to those made by 3 Corner Field Farm in Shushan, New York (sheep's milk, and more aged than Ardith Mae's, available through mail order); Lively Run Goat Dairy in Interlaken, New York (fresh and tangy, available through mail order and on the East Coast); Hidden Hills Boltenfeat in Everett, Pennsylvania (made from Jersey cow's milk); Amaltheia Dairy in Belgrade, Montana (goat's milk, widely available throughout the Northwest), and CKC Farms in Austin, Texas (goat's milk, mainly available in the South and Southwest).

Ochoa Cotija, Oregon

Francisco Ochoa's father, Froylan Ochoa, started making cheese in Oregon when his cravings for authentic Mexican-style queso frescos demanded that he either eat the mass-produced versions sold at grocery stores, or make his own. So the son of two cheesemakers got to work.

Word got around. The Ochoas went from making cheese for their family, to making it for their friends, to making it for friends of friends and cousins of friends, to finally opening shop in 2003. They became a go-to source for fresh Mexican-style cheeses in the Pacific North-west. Francisco, who took over the next year at age twenty after his father passed away, noticed that people were hankering for something stronger. Something saltier, firmer, drier. He determined they needed a queso seco or añejo to add another dimension to traditional dishes. In 2010, Ochoa added cotija to their repertoire to meet that demand.

The Ochoas' cotija comes in an inch-and-a-half-high cylinder. It's in the expansive queso seco or añejo family of cheeses—meaning dried or aged. It looks like many queso fresco until unwrapped, when its color shows up a little more buttery than the snow-white frescos sold here. When sliced, the cotija stays firm and crumbles only a tad around the edges. Cotija needs to be pressed lightly between the fingers to make the separate pieces that top dishes such as tostadas or enchiladas.

Traditionally intended to add a sharp, salty, vibrant taste the way Parmigiano-Reggiano flavors cooked dishes, cotija's taste is clean, creamy, sometimes nutty, and salty. Unlike many mass-produced versions, Ochoa's version uses whole rather than skim milk. Many big guys cut corners and costs by removing the cream, which Francisco says is "authentic and important," and as we know, really delicious. Ochoa also makes great effort to keep it simple in terms of cultures, using them to initiate acidification as opposed to building flavors that aren't in low-grade, pasteurized milk in the first place.

Referencing the way his grandmother and his mother made their cotija in Guadalajara (cotijas are made differently in many regions, one cotija being made only in the summer and fall in the mountain Michoacán town of Mexico), Ochoa crafts his cotija in as much of a traditional, regional manner as possible in the States. He starts off with pasteurized milk, as is legally mandated when making a cheese that is aged under sixty days (at the time of this writing, Ochoa is considering raw milk versions but isn't sure which direction his musings will take). In Mexico, where young raw milk cheeses are legal, they wouldn't need to add cultures because from the time they bring the unpasteurized morning milk from small towns to cheesemaking facilities, the ambient bacteria would already be working its acidification magic on the simple cheese, says Ochoa.

After adding cultures and rennet, it's time to cut the curds. But Ochoa doesn't use a machine or a classic cheese harp. Instead he uses large paddles that look like something to get pizza from an oven. "It's like the way I learned to make it at home," says Ochoa, "with a big, flat spoon." And he doesn't exactly "cut" the curds. He breaks up the curds with three or four slices, lets them sit for four to five minutes, then stirs the large curds until they break into little balls.

Once firm, the whey is drained and the curds are poured into blocks. He keeps piling the blocks one on top of another, which acts as a built-in press. When the curd is dry, Ochoa breaks it into little pieces and salts the curd. Next the curds are put in molds lined with cheesecloth and pressed in a machine press. According to Ochoa, this was when his mother would have put the cheese outside to dry and weighed it down with a rock. Here it stays under press for forty-eight hours, then is sent to a room to age for thirty days.

Then it's sent to local shops mainly on the West Coast. Traditionally, cotija is used in enchiladas and to top dishes such as beans or tostadas to add deeper flavors the way an aged Italian cheese would to ricotta in a lasagna, or ricotta salata would in salads. I like to use it as a substitute for ricotta salata at home or to add a salty, sharp kick to pastas or rice dishes, or crumbled over fried eggs. Pair with wine according to whatever it's cooked in; this is cheese meant to bring out the best in others.

If Ochoa's cheese can't be found near you, and you'd like a more aged cotija-style cheese, La Vaquita's queso fresco Salvadoreño (although it says it's a fresco, it's more aged than the average fresco, and has a sharper cotija bite) from Houston, Texas. But ask around. Many times the good, smaller production cotijas are available only at local shops.

Chilled Asparagus Watercress Soup
with Queso Fresco

Queso fresco's soft, fresh, milky flavors are the perfect highlight for this seasonal asparagus watercress soup. Make this in the spring, when asparagus are sweet and watercress is snappy yet tender. While I loved Narragansett's soft and crumbly queso blanco with the sweet asparagus, most local queso fresco will do. If in a pinch, chèvre also works. I don't strain my soup, but anyone looking for an especially silky consistency may do so.

1 tablespoon and 1 teaspoon butter
2 leeks, approximately 2 pounds
2 large garlic cloves, chopped fine
⅔ pound russet potatoes, peeled and large diced
1½ teaspoons salt
4½ cups stock
¾ pound asparagus
12 ounces watercress, large thick stems removed
3 tablespoons cream
3 tablespoons lemon juice
salt and pepper to taste
½ pound queso fresco

Slice off the bottoms of the leeks so that the vegetable's rings are revealed. Then cut off the top dark green part, 4–5 inches from the bottom. Dispose of the top and bottom. Slice the remaining leek lengthwise, then into half-rings about a half-inch thick. Wash under running water to get rid of any dirt or sand. Set aside to drain.

Trim the asparagus by cutting off the bottom inch of the stalks and discard. Cut the remaining stalks into inch-sized pieces. Set aside.

Bring a medium-sized soup pot to medium heat. Add the butter. When melted, add the leeks and garlic. Cook for 5–10 minutes, or until the leeks start to become translucent. Add potatoes and salt, and pour in the stock to cover the potatoes by an inch and a half. Add water if needed. Bring to a boil, then reduce to a simmer. Cook for 10–15 minutes, or until potatoes just give with a fork. Add asparagus and cook for 3–5 more minutes so that the asparagus are tender but still bright green. Add watercress, cook for 4–5 minutes more.

Transfer the soup in batches to a blender or food processer and blend until smooth. Strain now, if desired. Return to the pot, and add the cream and lemon juice. If too thick, add water two tablespoons at a time. Salt and pepper to taste. Chill.

Once chilled and ready to serve, crumble the queso fresco over each bowl and serve.

Goats, the Loire Valley, and Ash

• • • • •

Chèvre to a Higher Power

There's no other region in the world that's had as much influence on American goat cheese as France's Loire Valley. It's what Nashville, Tennessee, is to country music or what Victoria's Secret is to folks with a penchant for push-ups. An honored pilgrimage and reference site, the Loire Valley is where American goat's milk cheesemakers have looked most for inspiration. Their interpretation of its cheese styles in the nineties was very important—it helped to put our artisan cheese beyond chèvre on the map.

Loire Valley cheesemakers focus on small goat cheeses. Their specialties are soft, surface-ripened wheels or logs with rinds rippled like a morel mushroom. Some cheeses are off-white, cute, and very approachable. Others are dusted with vegetable ash that might send the wrong message if displayed next to Aunt Sally's urn at a memorial. Nearly all imported French goat cheeses sitting in an American cheesemonger's case, besides some from a few areas such as Provence, are from this region—Selles-sur-Cher, Crottin de Chavignol, Lingot de Quercy, St. Maure, and more.

Many of those credited with launching the "artisan cheese revolution," such as Mary Keehn of Cypress Grove in Humboldt, California; Allison Hooper of Vermont Butter & Cheese Creamery in Websterville, Vermont; and Judy Schad of Capriole in Greenville, Indiana, either educated themselves in the Loire or extensively studied their methods. These women (and the recent artisan cheese revolution *was* launched by women, as is explored thoroughly in Capriole's write-up in this section) started making fresh chèvre, then moved on to making their own versions of Crottins, Selles-sur-Cher, and beyond. Wabash Cannonball's or Goat Leap Eclipse's ash layers and lactic acid set style? Loire influenced. Vermont Butter & Cheese Creamery's Crottin? A Loire kissing cousin.

One reason this limestone-ridden area of France influenced so many American cheesemakers is because its products were already semimarketable here. Going with a style from an already familiar European region back in the eighties and nineties was the way to prove legitimacy. And gosh, if one of the five people familiar with the Loire classics picked up an American version one day instead of the Selles-sur-Cher to which they were accustomed, score. It also didn't hurt that these cheeses were simply delicious. "The Loire cheeses are wonderful," says Judy Schad. "They don't just taste good, they taste *great*. It took them three hundred years to get them that way, and they've got it."

Introducing small, lively Loire-inspired styles to Americans who were used to mild, bland flavors and becoming accustomed to the chèvre infiltration eased the nation past just Monterey Jack and cheddar blocks. In other words, it was an inspired way to expand palates beyond orange and white.

These cheeses are universally best with unoaked white wines and low oak reds such as Sauvignon Blanc or Cabernet Franc or Pinot Noir from the Loire Valley. Way to go, regional pairings!

Capriole Wabash Cannonball, Indiana

"Most of us came from cities," says Capriole owner Judy Schad of Greenville, Indiana, in reference to the handful of cheesemakers who taught people to rethink American artisan cheese. "Otherwise we wouldn't have done anything so stupid and think we could start our own farm or dairy. Any farmer could have told you that it was a bad idea. I probably thought I was canning tomatoes or making my own piecrust—I didn't know how truly complicated it was!"

We can be thankful that Schad went in . . . unaware. Without her and the other female pioneers digging blind in the trenches in the eighties and nineties, we might still be stuck in "yellow" cheese land. We'd also be without Capriole favorite Wabash Cannonball. It would be a sad life.

Specializing in Loire Valley–style goat cheeses made from the milk of their herd, Capriole makes the tiny three-ounce, ash-covered Wabash Cannonball. It's about the size of a golf ball and looks plush enough to cuddle. It's covered in a layer of gray ash that peeks through the soft, thin layer of white powdery mold covering the sphere. It's one of the prettiest cheeses you could put on a cheese plate. The texture is flaky and its taste is fresh, sweet, and citrusy.

Wabash Cannonball is the perfect vehicle for the goat's milk that Schad learned to master from the people she says really started the artisan cheese revolution in the United States—Letty and Bob Kilmoyer, former owners of Westfield Farm in Hubbardston, Massachusetts. Before Shad sampled Letty's chèvre, the city girl had no idea what to do with her farm's goat's milk. "When I ate her cheese," says Schad, "I finally knew what this milk was for."

We should consider ourselves lucky that Schad's eldest son brought a goat into the family's life for a 4-H project. After they found the first goat so charming, the family got another. And then another. Described by many women as the ultimate female animal, says Schad, goats embody all the things that make women intriguing. This is why she thinks so many female cheesemakers were drawn to them.

"Goats are charming in ways others are not. They're interesting, they do bad things, they eat all your rosebushes, they can open doors and latches, and they're really smart survivors. You can't help but respect them."

It was a handful of female cheesemakers who brought goat cheese into people's homes in the eighties and nineties in the United States. Through their work they exposed American palates to cheeses they had never heard of and animal's milk that they didn't know could be made into cheese. It was their cheese, not the large-production ones made mostly by men in large factories, which brought creditability to the American artisan cheese movement. This isn't a surprise to some such as Schad.

Cheesemaking originally was mainly woman's work. Husbands would care for the land and animals, and the wives would make cheese in their kitchen. The women would make cheese for the household and some extra for the market to augment the farm income. Once men saw that selling cheese in the market was a successful venture, they consolidated the milk supply, pooled the milk, and went commercial, outsourcing the female craft.

"When we started making cheese, it was a time of rethinking the food system and going back to the land," says Schad. "Things went full circle."

Chèvre was the first step. Moving on to more complex styles was the second. Still, it took time to perfect creations such as Wabash.

The standard rind for soft cheeses at the time was a bloomy rind like that covering Cowgirl Creamery's Mt. Tam. Schad fooled around with it, yet found Wabash too itty-bitty to handle such a big rind. Without any American inspirations for rind options, Schad didn't know what to do. Luckily, it wasn't long before Schad spotted the perfect sheath.

The International Goat Association Conference takes place every four years, and that year, it just happened to be in the Loire, and Schad just happened to be asked to judge the St. Maure cheese section. Downright delicious, these goat cheeses used the *Geotrichum candidum* mold for their wrinkly rinds, were ashed, and were made of small-batch goat's milk. They were what pushed Schad to go Loire in her cellar. She hooked up with celebrated cheesemaker and scholar Sister Noella Marcellino, aka the Cheese Nun, who happened to be doing a Fulbright on *Geotrichum candidum* in France, and the sister taught her how to work with the wrinkled, brainy mold at home.

Capriole perfected Wabash Cannonball in 1992. To make Wabash, Capriole starts out with Capriole's standard chèvre base, rolls it into three-ounce balls, then lets it ripen overnight. The next day, they roll it in a French ash—but not too much.

"Mary Keehn and I have a saying," says Schad. "'A little ash goes a long way.'"

Following the ashing, they cellar the immature Wabash. One to two weeks later a powdery white rind develops. That's when they ship it out. They know that within a week or two, the *Geo* will start showing its wrinkly self.

As with other Loire Valley cheeses, think Loire grapes—Sauvignon Blanc, Muscadet, Chenin Blanc, Cabernet Franc, and Pinot Noir. Some other ash-coated *Geotrichum* beauties to try are Prodigal Farm's Hunkadora from Rougemont, North Carolina; Asgaard Farm's Barkeater Bouche (a firmer style shaped like the Loire Valley St. Maure log) from Au Sable Forks, New York; Vermont Butter & Cheese's Bonne Bouche (a flat disk) from Websterville, Vermont (widely available); Shamrocks's Ashed Tommette from Willits, California (available online); and Lazy Lady's Valençay from Westfield, Vermont (available mainly on the East Coast).

Vermont Butter & Cheese Creamery Bijou, Vermont

Bijou was the first in a line of Vermont Butter & Cheese Creamery's surface-ripened, Loire Valley–style goat cheeses that originally helped introduce Americans to aged goat cheese. After Americans became accustomed to chèvre in salads or crumbling it on sun-dried tomato pizzas, they were ready to open their hearts to a more complex Loire Valley–inspired gem.

Cheeses such as Bijou upped the ante. Bijou, a soft cheese with a light white, rippled rind, is Vermont Butter & Cheese Creamery's tiniest aged goat. It is an homage to the Loire Valley's famed Crottin de Chavignol and the tiny rippled cheeses stacked in French outdoor markets.

Bijou starts out very mild. Its wavy rind comes paper-thin and smudges if nudged, and its flavors are as light, fresh, and lemony as a chèvre. As it ages, its rind grows to a thicker yet still delicate snowy beige, and although it never loses its taste of fresh cream, its grassy flavors become more pronounced and peppery. In France, they melt this style over toasted bread for chèvre chaud and consume the cheese with vigor at various stages of life—from young and pert to nearly rock hard and completely covered with mold.

Bijou is made like the Loire crottins that inspired it. Cultures, enzymes, rennet, and molds are added to the fresh, pasteurized milk and then lactose is left to convert to lactic acid overnight. This is called a lactic acid set. Now fairly common, the method was so unusual when cheesemaker Allison Hooper started using it in the late nineties that it perplexed the engineers developing her aged cheese. "They had this look on their faces," she recalls, "that said something like, 'This isn't how you make cheddar.'" Leaving the milk to acidify overnight is a traditional practice with many softer cheeses—Loire included. The curds need less rennet to solidify and the cheese can develop a fresh, tangy edge.

After the curds are set, they're gently pumped into traditional French cheese bags and stacked one atop another so that the liquid (the whey) can drain from the proteins and fat. Such is typical of many French crottins, too. Allowing the whey to drain with only this light pressure allows Bijou to keep its creamy texture—more moisture remains in the curd. Twenty-four hours later, the stacked curds are taken from the bags, shaped into two-ounce pieces, put on racks, and sent to the cave with the other aged cheeses.

While in the cave, Bijou takes on more characteristics of a surface-ripened waved rind. The *Geotrichum candidum* mold (the one that ripples all the famous brainy cheese—La Tur, crottins, etc.) that was added to the milk starts to do its thing, creating a thin rind that will later wrinkle if left alone.

"We love the brainy look," Vermont Butter & Cheese Creamery co-owner Bob Reese says. "We rave about it the more wrinkled it is."

The company has a lot to rave about. Along with a few female goat cheese makers across the country in the eighties and nineties, cheesemaker Allison Hooper helped put goat cheese on American tables at a time when people, mainly men, were pumping out commodity cheddar or Jack. Perhaps because goat's milk has never been available in the United States in large supply, the cheeses still remain artisanal. Whatever it is, Vermont Butter & Cheese Creamery's make room stays small, and the quality has remained as good as, if not better than, when they first started.

Regional pairings work best with this Loire Valley–style cheese. Look to the vineyards in France. The grapes of the Loire Valley region—Sauvignon Blanc, Chenin Blanc, Melon de Bourgogne, Cabernet Franc, and Pinot Noir—love a Bijou right. They have enough acidity to match the cheese's liveliness and citrus flavors and lack oak or heavy oaking that often clash with a *Geotrichum candidium*–influenced rind.

Some other great crottin-style cheeses to taste are Redwood Hill's Crottin from Sebastapol, California; Capriole's Crocodile Tear from Greenville, Indiana; and River's Edge's Valsetz from Logsden, Oregon. Most are widely available nationwide.

Goat's Leap Eclipse, California

Goat's Leap owners Barbara and Rex Backus in Napa Valley bought their first fifty-gallon milk pasteurizer in 1992. They still have it. At the height of their production, they might fill the vat with thirty-five gallons of milk three times a week to craft no more than one hundred pounds of cheese total.

That said, Eclipse is one of the hardest to find of their already rare and delicious cheeses. I buy it as soon as I see it—even if the two elderly ladies behind me at the cheese shop are giving me the evil eye, or if the mother of the baby in the carriage next to me wanted that to be her child's first bite of goat's milk cheese. First in line means first in line.

"We never had any intention of getting bigger," says Barbara. "We

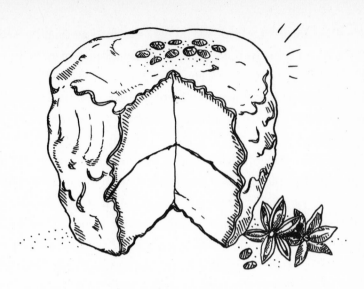

Goat's Leap Eclipse

always wanted to stay small because that was what was best for our property, animals, and cheese. In our warped head, that was our business plan. Of course," laughs Barbara, "we didn't share that with the bank."

Barbara has been making Eclipse since the early nineties. Their bestselling cheese, Eclipse is a three-inch cylinder covered in a thin bloomy white rind over a light ash dusting. It's topped with star anise pieces like cherries on a sundae and its center is pure white, cut with a strip of thin ash that sits like frosting on the first layer of a birthday cake. The anise flavor seeps delicately into the paste, adding just a touch of spiced sweetness to the already sweet and lightly tangy milk. Underneath the rind, a thin velvety cheese layer acts like piece of silk on the tongue and grows thicker toward the flaky center as it ages.

Although inspired by the Loire in production and premise, Eclipse has a typically American characteristic. That is the uber-popular goat cheese bloomy rind that came into fashion in the United States with

Cypress Grove's Humboldt Fog. Mainly an American thing, this sort of bloomy rind is seen on few goat Frenchies that make it to the United States, with the exception of Bucheron. The French goat cheeses that make it here are generally *Geotrichum candidum* mold, brainy styles, and the *Penicillium candidum* rinds adheres mainly to cow's milk.

But when American cheesemakers realized that they couldn't use raw milk like the Loire did, says Backus, many thought their milk would be compromised and they started looking outside the normal-rind box. They wanted something to add flavor to their subdued milk after pasteurization, like a bloomy rind. Then, many went for the ash for another boost. Ash, typical in the Loire Valley, helps the bloomy rind to develop. It also helped a large-format goat cheese such as Eclipse ripen. Sprinkling a mixture of ash and salt between the curd layers ages the center by changing the cheese's pH, and leeches out even more whey. Plus, it made it as pretty as a birthday cake when sliced into.

Like the Bijou, Eclipse is a lactic-acid-set cheese. It's left over-night, then the curd is ladled into a perforated tray covered with cheesecloth to drain. The thin ash line is added when the curd is la-dled a second time into molds. After the cheese is left to drain for between twenty-four and thirty-six hours (depending on the humid-ity and weather), it's transferred to a rack to dry and ash is patted on the outside. If the *Penicillium candidum* mold hasn't formed by then, a tray is flipped over to make a cover for the baby Eclipses to speed up the process. Then it's sent to the fridge and wrapped to go a week later.

Even though a taste of Eclipse might suggest otherwise, like many cheesemakers who start out as dairy farmers or breeders, the Backuses realized that their first love was the goats. The cheese came twenty years later because they wanted to honor their animals by using their milk on the farm. Barbara's glad she did, but she doesn't think they'd be making cheese if they didn't own their animals.

"I saw goats at a petting zoo doing goaty things, and I was enchanted," she says. "They're naughty, they tear down fences, and they give you kisses."

Think Loire for the pairings here, too, as with Bijou. It's okay to diverge from the region's grapes, but think fresh and unoaked for whites. Stay away from tannic or oaky reds completely, though—they conflict with the rind and the flavors get harsher as the cheese ages.

Other bloomy rinded and ashed cheeses to try if you fall in love with Eclipse, want to try more, or can't find it near you are Rainbow Ridge's Lil Bloomy (without ash) from Bedford Hills, New York; Ardith Mae's Bigelow from Hallstead, Pennsylvania (ash rind); Prodigal Farm's Hunkadora from Rougemont, North Carolina (ash rind); and Andante Accapella from Sonoma, California (ash rind). All are very limited, but worth seeking out. And of course, there is always Cypress Grove's Humboldt Fog, available nationwide, which is also cut through the center with ash like Eclipse.

English Pea and Herb Purée
for Loire Valley–Style Goat Cheese

SERVES 4–5

This quick purée is a perfect go-to for lightly aged goat cheese. It's especially good with the hint of star anise that tops the Eclipse cheese, but the chervil, parsley, and lemon juice in the spread match well with the seasonal flavors in any Loire-inspired goat cheese. It tastes best when spread over grilled bread drizzled with olive oil, toasted crostini, or crackers. I used frozen, shelled organic peas for my version, but you're more than welcome to use fresh. If using fresh peas, shell them and blanch them in salted boiling water for three to five minutes until they're tender but still bright green. Then dunk them in an ice bath, and drain. Use any leftover purée on sandwiches the next day.

½ bunch chervil, large stems removed
⅓ cup loosely packed parsley leaves
1 small garlic clove, roughly chopped
1 (10-ounce) bag frozen green peas, brought to
　　room temperature
2 tablespoons olive oil
1 tablespoon lemon juice, freshly squeezed
⅛ teaspoon salt
salt and pepper to taste
bruschetta, crostini, or crackers to serve
2 ounces room-temperature Eclipse goat cheese
　　per person

Add the chervil, parsley, and garlic to a food processor and pulse for 1–2 minutes until the herbs are well chopped. Add the remaining ingredients and blend for 2–3 minutes until you have a purée with an easy-to-spread consistency. Salt and pepper to taste—remember that the cheese will have its own salt, so season modestly.

If using a blender to combine, add all ingredients to the base and blend 2–3 minutes, adding alternating half-tablespoons of extra virgin olive oil and water until the puree blends easy.

To serve, spread on bruschetta, crostini, or crackers. Top with a half-ounce of Eclipse per serving.

Creamy and Soft

• • • • •

Crèmes and Butter

It's no surprise that creamy cheeses fly off the shelves faster than warm chocolate chip cookies fresh from the oven. As seductive as Marilyn Monroe walking over a subway grate and as comforting as a purring kitten, creamy cheeses are irresistible—folks can't help loving them.

They appeal to our subconscious survival instincts with rich, sweet flavors that suggest they could keep whoever's eating them alive through multiple New England blizzards. They appeal to our emotional sides by tasting like the butter we used to spread thickly on our toast as children before "calorie" entered our vocabulary and like the ice cream that comforts us when eaten from the container.

These white bloomy-rinded, soft-ripening wheels of seduction originated in Northern France in areas such as Normandy, where Camembert and the first double crème were created. Nowhere will you find a cheese with as much ooey-gooey oomph as you will in the land of butter and cream—France. Well, except here. Have we talked about how much Americans love sweet, lush things yet?

The creamies that have made their mark the most here are those that have been inoculated with *Penicillium candidum* and maybe a little *Geotrichum candidum* mold to help develop their soft, plush, white rinds and centers. They're soft-ripening cheeses (they become softer as they age) and sometimes look meltier around the rind than they do in the center because they ripen from the outside in.

Some double or triple crèmes such as Sweet Grass's Green Hill, featured in this chapter, or Cowgirl Creamery's Mt. Tam, are either made entirely of cream or have cream added to the milk base to make them taste even richer. These are classified as double or triple crèmes according to their butterfat content (but because only the dry matter is measured in these moist cheeses during fat count, they actually have less fat than officially recorded). Others are just creamy via production. Keeping curds large, for example, keeps the cheese moisture content high, and the milk of certain cow breeds can add more lushness, too.

Because they automatically score points in the cheese case due to familiarity, and appeal to cheese lovers and novices alike due to general deliciousness, it doesn't take much to inspire a cheesemaker to try their hand at a butterbomb. Except, well, they're actually hard to make. These easy pleasers are actually cheese princesses in disguise. If their curds aren't properly coddled from the time they coagulate to the time they hit the shops, and if they're not kept in perfectly humidified and temperate aging areas, they throw a fit and refuse to hold their shape and texture.

Like all the royalty I know, creamy cheeses are huge fans of Champagne and sparkling wine. They're New Year's Eve parties waiting to happen. Unlike princesses, they promise to stay and love you once the clock strikes midnight.

Scholten Family Farm Weybridge, Vermont

Almost entirely black except for a two-foot-wide white stripe wrapping around their stomachs, the Scholtens' Dutch belted cows look like chocolate cream sandwich cookies. And they're proud of it. Leaving behind the few Holsteins who didn't quite make the team, they saunter around the field like a clique of high school girls who just learned they all made the cheerleading squad.

That the Scholten family makes a cheese called Weybridge from the organic milk of their Dutch belteds in Middlebury, Vermont, only provides more fuel to the heritage breed's ego fire. Around an inch tall and barely reaching six ounces, Weybridge is smooth, soft, and covered in a plush rind reminiscent of fake Christmas snow. It has an opulent, rich paste and can taste of fresh porcini mushrooms and sesame butter.

Even though it's a single crème, meaning it clocks in under 45 percent butterfat, Weybridge could fool any onlooker into thinking

Scholten Weybridge

it's made of creamier stuff. Pan in to the smiling Scholtens and the proud Dutch belteds.

When owners Patty and Roger Scholten were deciding what cheese to make, they started from the ground up—they asked cheese-mongers what people wanted. The answer was a creamy, bloomy-rinded cheese that could take on similar styles from France. Because the Scholtens' push to make cheese stemmed from a desire to stop selling all their milk to large processors, they needed their cheese to propel their family of six forward financially. So they took the mon-gers' advice to heart and went a step further by choosing heritage cows, too.

Brought to North America from the Netherlands in 1838, Dutch belteds have a relatively high butterfat content to their milk (just under Jerseys) and tiny fat globules that bind exceptionally well to proteins so that less butterfat is lost during the cheesemaking process. The Scholtens knew that using a heritage breed with distinct milk composition and flavor profiles would make a creamy cheese even better (and those cute white Dutch belted cow belts couldn't hurt with marketing either).

To make Weybridge, the Scholtens first milk their cows with music. The cows are milked twice a day, and according to Roger, who is in charge of cow caretaking, they're lulled into milking with clas-sical music in the morning—"when rock is too much"—and intro-duced to AC/DC in the day.

After pasteurization, sole cheesemaker Patty adds *Penicillium can-didum* mold (along with rennet and cultures) to the milk. This is when the bloomy rind magic happens. *Penicillium candidum* goes into every bloomy rind cheese from Brie to Cowgirl Creamery's Mt. Tam to Weybridge. It is what covers the wheels in the plush white rind, and it encourages the wheels to soften from the center out as they age and become creamy mounds.

Once the milk starts to coagulate, Patty cuts large curds. Large curds mean there is less surface area for whey to expel, and the final cheese stays moister. She then pours the curds into plastic molds so wheels can form—pouring instead of hand ladling takes less time and enables Patty, who works by herself, to make more cheese.

After keeping the cheese for a week, the Scholtens ship the cheese to Jasper Hill Cellars in Greensboro, Vermont. There, Weybridge finishes maturing. When the Scholtens got into cheesemaking, Patty knew she'd need help. She stalked (her words) the Kehler brothers of Jasper Hill until they agreed to help her refine the make and finish aging Weybridge in their cellar so she could focus on running the farm, making more cheese, and telling those Dutch belteds how pretty they are every day.

When pairing Weybridge to wine, I generally skip red altogether. The molds in the rind, especially as the cheese ages, can have tiny battles with the red fruit of the wine in your mouth and get in the way of a smooth pairing experience. Gamays, Nebbiolos, and some Pinot Noirs work, but white is easier. I go for slightly nutty, earthy whites with good acidity such as Chardonnays from Burgundy or the Jura region to match like flavors in the cheese. I also love this cheese with a dry sherry or brown ales.

Here are a few other soft single to double crèmes to try, too: Baby Caprino by CKC Farms in Blanco, Texas (made with goat's milk, limited distribution nationwide); Nicasio's Fromagella from Nicascio, California (limited distribution nationwide); Branched Oak's Prairie Breeze from Lancaster, Nebraska (hard to find, but becoming more widely available); and Lazy Lady Farm's goat-cow Demi Tasse from Westfield, Vermont (limited availability).

Sweet Grass Dairy Green Hill, Georgia

It seems appropriate that one of reasons Sweet Grass Dairy's cheese-maker Jeremy Little, the creator of one of the creamiest, most lovable double crèmes around, turned to cheese was because he wants people to learn to celebrate life. Like a grandmother baking her eleventh batch of holiday cookies, double crèmes are all about spreading the love. They do it well on a cracker, with a bottle of bubbly, and most certainly on a date with crusty bread and salami.

Everyone likes a plush little butter pillow. When the pillow exudes more flavor notes than just butter and salt (like *some* unnamable French triple crèmes), the feeling shifts from like to adoration.

Sweet Grass's Green Hill is such a cheese pillow. A disk around an inch high and an inch-and-a-half thick, depending on who ladled the curds into the molds, Green Hill is covered with a thin, soft white bloomy rind that screams, *"Touch me!"* When sliced into, the rind gives as if you're passing a knife through frosting and the French vanilla–colored center shines like room-temperature butter. The taste is buttery, mushroom-like, with hints of untoasted, sweet young walnut, and the grass the Littles' Jersey cows feed on.

As is true in any true double crème, the Littles add cream to their milk to intensify the decadent experience, but part of Green Hill's glory comes from the grass and their particular cows.

Jeremy Little and his wife, Jessica Wehner, took over Sweet Grass in Thomasville, Georgia, from Jessica's parents in 2005. Jessica's father, who calls himself a "grass farmer," was one of the first to bring the practice of rotational grazing back into the dairy world in the 1990s. Years later, Jessica's mother started Sweet Grass because, rather than ship their pastured Jersey milk off to be mixed in a tank with milk from cows who saw less grass than Richard Nixon in the sixties, she wanted to feature it in a product that would show how exceptional it was.

Says cook-cum-cheesemaker Jeremy Little, "It's all about the raw ingredients." Then, it's about doing the little things to highlight those ingredients. To get the cream for Green Hill, for example, Little puts his milk in a tank and lets the cream rise to the top instead of using a mechanical agitator to separate the two that could damage the milk structure. Then he slowly pumps out the milk, puts it aside for other Sweet Grass, lower-in-fat cheese, and uses the cream to start a batch of Green Hill.

After pasteurizing the cream, he adds enzymes, cultures, and everyone's favorite *Penicillium candidum* mold, which makes the rind bloomy. Next, he adds the rennet. Little says it's a judgment call when the curd is ready, but he often uses a cake spatula to see if the curd is properly coagulated. When the curd grabs on to the spatula, it's ready to go. Then he cuts the curds into pieces "smaller than half-dollars, but bigger than quarters," stirs them by hand, and lightly heats them in order to firm. He then ladles the curds by hand into the molds in three layers until they're full. He flips Green Hill twice in the next three hours to distribute moisture, drains them overnight, and salts them. Two weeks and several flippings later, Green Hill is sent to a cheese shop near you—but it doesn't stay there for long.

Like many double crèmes, Green Hill practically hops into shopping bags. It's Sweet Grass's biggest seller. Little credits the popularity to the cheese's familiarity. "It's not a cheese investment," he says, "it's safe. It has a bloomy rind, it looks like Brie. It helps people get through the buying process when there's so much selection."

That explains the initial draw, but Green Hill's depth of flavor speaks for itself. Then, it's all over once the bubbles come out. Beer and wine drinker Little says he's never had a better pairing for his creamy one than Champagne, which makes sense since a Champagne's nutty and brioche-like flavors mimic the buttery yeastiness of Green Hill. For a little extra celebration, Little suggests enjoying with peach preserves (he likes American Spoon's from Georgia) or with sesame crackers.

If you're a fan of this double crème, which is pretty easy to find in the United States, here are a few other double and triples to seek out: Cowgirl Creamery's Mt. Tam from Point Reyes, California; Vermont Butter & Cheese Creamery's Crèmont from Websterville, Vermont (goat and cow blend); and Nettle Meadow's Three Sisters from Warrensburg, New York (goat, cow, and sheep blend). Most are widely available.

Kurtwood Farms Dinah, Washington

Before making Dinah, Kurt Timmermeister opened one of Seattle's first coffee shop and bakeries in an instance of impeccable timing— he and Starbucks opened the same year and "coffee culture" became a phrase. Later, once he was making Dinah, a literary agent who just happened to have been reading his monthly newsletters about his farm and dairy approached him and suggested he write a book. *Growing a Farmer* was also a success.

Except for that unfortunate two-or-three-year stretch when he tried to farm organic vegetables for a living and ended up with more problems than profit, cheesemaker, baker, restaurateur, and writer Kurt Timmermeister seems to have a blessed touch. And for this we are thankful.

Timmermeister's first cheese is named after his first cow and now retired milker, Dinah. It's a seven-to-eight-ounce disk with a bloomy rind made with the butterfat-rich milk of his twelve-Jersey herd and now includes Dinah 2.0. Made in the Camembert style, Dinah is a little more delicate than the archetype. It tastes like sweet milk, mushrooms, and cream. "It's super rich," says Timmermeister, "and sometimes I think kids like it more than adults." When it starts out, it is very mild and has a chalky center. As it ages, it becomes gooey and a little bit more pungent. A few days later, when it starts to eye that hill it will go over in a week, it begins to liquefy.

Timmermeister knows he's been lucky. But he's also a nice guy and a hard worker who admits to failing daily. The morning we spoke, he discovered he could cure three weeks' worth of rind problems by just adding a space heater to his ripening room. So it feels right to consider his blessings *our* blessings.

To make Dinah, he starts out with pasteurized milk. After pasteurization, Timmermeister drops the temperature to around ninety degrees, adds cultures, *Penicillium candidum* and *Geotrichum candidum* molds for rind and paste development, and lets everything marinate. A couple hours later he adds rennet, lets the curd come to the right consistency, then cuts them into to ¾-inch squares. Ten minutes later he hand ladles them into molds, drains, and flips them. Later in the evening he unmolds them.

When they're firm and look like hockey pucks, he salts them, drains them again, then loads them into racks that go into a cooler for six to seven days where the bloomy mold can start growing. When they start to bloom, Timmermeister wraps them in paper and moves them to a lower-temperature room to ripen for two to three weeks. Then he delivers them at whatever ripeness he wants—he's the only person who delivers them to local spots, so he can make sure they're exactly how he wants them.

The self-taught learner admits that it's taken a while to get them that way. "There are far better cheesemakers than me," he says. "I've thrown away a thousand dollars' worth of cheese before because the paste was too ripe." Perhaps, but high-moisture cheeses such as Dinah are notoriously fussy, prone to falling apart in skilled and noviced hands. The high moisture content makes it so the curd can break anytime, even during transportation from cheesemaker to shop, and it makes them good homes to bad bacteria that can mess with the wheel's texture, rind, and flavor. As millions of creamy cheese lovers admit, after a cheesemaker has thrown away enough bad ones to know just how to make the good ones right, there's nothing like a good, buttery Camembert-style wedge.

Serve Dinah with a bubbly, Chardonnay (oaked or unoaked), or a Rhone blend such as a Marsanne-Roussane-Grenache Blanc. If serving with reds, be cautious of the rind. It conflicts with the red fruit flavors in many reds and isn't a fan of tons of oak or tannin. Pinot, Gamays, and Cabernet Francs are all good choices, as are wit beers.

Some other must-try Camembert styles (you might have to make a trip to the Pacific Northwest to taste Dinah) are Chapel Hill Creamery's Carolina Moon from Chapel Hill, North Carolina (also a little hard to find outside of the area); Del Cielo by Pure Luck Dairy in Dripping Springs, Texas (goat's milk, available in Texas, and through Houston Dairymaids, a Houston cheese shop that might ship if you ask nicely); Alemar's Bent River from Mankato, Minnesota (a little more strongly flavored, available on a small scale, nationwide); and Old Chatham's Nancy's Camembert from Old Chatham, New York (sheep and cow's milk, pretty easy to find).

Sesame-Almond Rosemary Crackers

MAKES 30–40 CRACKERS

This recipe was meant to play on the sesame flavors in Scholten's Wey-bridge, but will work for any creamy cheese in this book or beyond. The recipe was inspired by one of my favorite gluten-free blogs, Elana's Pantry. The cracker offers a crunchy contrast to the cheese's softness and the rosemary provides a little spice to liven up a creamy cheese. It's best if you use a food processor to grind half the sesame seeds in the recipe to the right consistency, but the crackers will be just fine if you mix the sesame seeds into the almond flour. Almond flour is available at most health food and grocery stores.

¼ cup white sesame seeds
1½ cups almond flour
¼ cup black sesame seeds
1 teaspoon kosher salt
1 egg, whisked well
1 tablespoon melted butter
¼ teaspoon chopped rosemary

Preheat oven to 350 degrees.

Pulse the white sesame in a food processor until around half of the seeds are ground into a sesame meal, 1–2 minutes.

Add the ground sesame meal, almond flour, black sesame seeds, and salt to a mixing bowl. Stir until well combined. Add the egg, melted butter, and rosemary and stir until combined. Form the dough into a rectangle.

Place a piece of parchment paper the size of a 12- by 16-inch baking sheet on a flat surface. Put the dough rectangle in the center of the parchment. Place another piece of parchment paper of equal size over the dough. Roll the dough out between the sheets, making sure to center the dough on the first sheet of parchment. When the dough is rolled to around an ⅛-inch thickness, move it and the bottom layer of parchment paper to a baking sheet. Cut the dough on the sheet into 1½-inch squares.

Bake for 10–15 minutes until the edges of the crackers start to turn golden.

Let cool, then break apart into the scored squares.

Mixed Milk

· · · · ·

Do the Animals Just Hang Out Together?

Depression Era grandmothers who saved their pennies in glass jars and found a second use for their old sweaters would be proud of mixed milk cheeses. Mixed milk cheeses make do with what the cheese lord provides them. Made of blends of cow, sheep, and goat's milk, they come in varying textures and flavors. Smart, sensible, and undeniably tasty like that bacon grease Grandma saved for frying eggs, they're as down home as they are modern.

Mixed milk cheese came to be in places such as Europe because families often had more than just one animal type in their barn, for milk, meat, clothing, and farming—and most females gave milk. When housewives had fulfilled their milk needs for the day, whether it be setting some aside for the family or making cheeses for market, they would often have odd amounts of leftover milk of varying animal types. Rather than waste it, many mixed it to make cheese. Some also intentionally mixed certain milks, like sheep's with goat's, because sheep's milk coagulated easier and would aid the cheesemaking process.

Of course, now people make mixed milks for many reasons. For some, it's still a matter of simply using what one can get. Sheep's milk is hard to come by, for example, so in order to use at least some of their preferred milk, some cheesemakers will make mixed wheels out of necessity. Others make mixed milks when one type of animal isn't providing as much milk as the other because of breeding seasons.

Then there's the fact that mixing milks and, hence, flavors, is fun, not always just necessary. Quite simply, when a cheesemaker mixes milks, they get the best of whatever milk worlds they're mixing. Coagulation might be easier, sure, but the flavor combination of sheep and goat make a bang-up cheese with all the nutty, brown buttery flavors of sheep's milk mixed with the lively herbal flavors of goat's milk. Not bad.

Making a mixed milk cheese helps a cheese stand out in a crowd beyond its flavor profile, too, because mixed milks are still unique. As more folks make more artisan cheese and expand the artisan milk market possibilities, more milk types will be widely available. As more become readily available, cheesemakers will start crafting more mixed cheese. But as it is now, finding extra milks (especially non–cow's milk) isn't always easy. Hence the rare wheel with a picture of a cow and a goat on it will always draw the consumer's attention in a packed cheese case.

Which brings me to another point. No, Mr. Smarty Pants snickering in the back of a cheese class, there exists no tin-can-eating goat-sheep-cow hybrid with fuzzy, black-and-white-spotted wool that supplies the milk for these cheeses. Inventive cheesemakers (you know, the ones with original jokes) make these beauties all on their own.

Hidden Springs Meadow Melody, Wisconsin

Drive up the small winding Westby roads to Hidden Springs, and you'll discover one of the only licensed sheep's cheesemaking creameries in the United States that uses donkeys as bodyguards. In the middle of Wisconsin Amish country, cheesemaker Brenda Jenson does things the old-fashioned way, tilling the land by hand with draft horses and protecting her sheep from predators with animals that have a fierce back kick.

The main reason for making Meadow Melody is as based in tradition as the buggies treading the local roads. Like many cheesemakers before her, Jenson wanted a way to bulk up her cheese production in the summer, when sheep produce less milk as their bodies preserve energy. Solution? Do a little extracurricular milk mixing with a

meadow melody

nearby cow herd. A savvy little bonus? As Jenson knew before mixing 51 percent of her neighbors cow's milk with 49 percent of her own sheep's milk, the Wisconsin Milk Marketing Board (funded by cow's milk dairy farmers) heavily promotes creameries making cheese that are at least half cow's milk. A cheesemaker can always use a little help.

This blend of cow's and sheep's milk sits about two-and-a-half inches tall and has a Dijon mustard–hued rind and creamy off-white interior. Semifirm, the smooth and easily meltable cheese is modeled after Hidden Spring's Ocooch Mountain sheep's milk wheel, which was modeled after the French Savoie region's Abondance (both rock in fondue or raclette). It has a bright, gentle grassy and sweet butterscotch cream flavor with a slight tang—a great intro to sheep's milk cheese and a respite for cow's milk cheese lovers.

Beyond being a great cheese for the creamery because it appeals to everyone from cheese sophisticates to teenagers, Meadow Melody makes more sense for Hidden Springs than a pair of black low-heeled pumps does for a middle-aged businesswoman. It helps to buff out sheep's summer cheese milk, it garners promotion from the state's powerhouse marketing team, which is extremely helpful for a small cheesemaker (Jenson made a faux label that says, "Hidden Springs and Milk Marketing Machine, True Love Forever"), and it requires very little additional labor to start making it even though it was an entirely new cheese. And it's delicious? My practical heart beats quicker just thinking about it.

Made in the model of another one of Jenson's cheeses so she didn't have to work months on perfecting another recipe or worry about a new mold transferring from wheel to wheel in the cheese cave, Meadow Melody is a kissing cousin of Ocooch Mountain.

Jenson starts by cooling the cow's and sheep's milk, which come to the creamery at animal body temperature together. After pasteurization, Jenson adds her cultures and rennet and lightly heats and stirs the developing curds. As with most other Alpine-style cheeses, the Meadow Melody curds are gathered and pressed in forms under whey—this helps to develop lactic acid and reduce holes in the paste. Then it's removed from liquid and again pressed overnight and salted. During the next three to five months, Meadow Melody is washed with a saltwater brine and housed in Jenson's caves—in the remodeled basement of the property's former house—before it hits the market.

Once it hits the market, it's everyone's best friend. It melts well, it tastes delicious at room temperature, and it loves nuts and jamon and mustard or prosciutto. It also likes white wines with low oak such as Chablis or Verdicchio, medium-bodied reds, and light and Belgian beers.

A few similar like-minded semifirm mixed milks to try after Meadow Melody are Haystack Mountain's Buttercup from Longmont, Colorado (cow and goat); Carr Valley Benedictine and Cave Aged Mellage (sheep, cow, and goat) from La Valle, Wisconsin; and Wisconsin Sheep Dairy's Mona (sheep and cow) from Catawba, Wisconsin (the Wisconsin ones are a little more readily available).

Délice de la Vallée Fromage Blanc, California

For years, Chef Sheana Davis's catering clients had been demanding so much of her house-made mixed milk fromage blanc that she was making anywhere from twenty-five to fifty pounds a week. This was good. But she never meant to go big with it.

All changed when a visiting health inspector told Davis that she was making so much cheese that she technically counted as a full-blown cheesemaking operation. The law said that if she wanted to keep legally making her clients' favorite dish, she needed to get certi-fied and move her cheese operation from her tiny catering kitchen to a licensed cheesemaking facility, pronto. So Davis decided that since she had to invest to churn out her beloved cheese in a larger facility, she might as well make enough Délice de la Vallée to get it past the buffet table and into home kitchens. High-five, health inspector.

Translating to "delight of the valley," Délice is an uber-crèmed fromage blanc, or as Davis likes to call it, a "crème de fromage." It's a triple crème, fresh, soft cheese made with whole cow's milk and cream, with fresh Sonoma chèvre mixed in.

Most American fromage blancs are made from whole cow's milk, are lovely and lightly creamy, and are tantalizing enough in their freshness alone. But Davis pushes boundaries (leave it to a power-house ex–roller derby skater to take a cheese to its limits). A spread-able, fluffy white cheese with small grains, Délice tastes like sweet cow's cream drizzled with a touch of melted butter and squeeze of grassy lemon.

Davis starts with raw cow's milk that she buys from her local Sonoma milk pool. Like her friend, Bleating Heart's Seana Doughty (later profiled in this book), Davis doesn't own any animals. Of course, running her catering company and gourmet retail shop keeps her a little busy, but beyond that, she just doesn't want to.

"I don't have any desire to have animals, I'm cool with buying milk from hardworking farmers at their price point and helping to form relationships so they can stay alive. I'm proud of that."

Once the mainly organic milk hits the cheesemaking facilities she rents, Davis pasteurizes it; adds cream, cultures, and rennet; and in a similar fashion to Salvatore ricotta, lets it rest and drain overnight. The next morning she stirs in the chèvre. Then she ships 30 percent of her Délice to Brooklyn. Because only vegetarian rennet is used,

Délice is a popular fromage blanc among Jewish East Coasters seeking a little fresh kosher dairy action.

As a fresh cheese, Délice is meant to be consumed quickly. Davis says that even though it could last eight weeks, she likes it best at four. But it never lasts that long—all is gone within a week, having been sent to the East Coast, sold at local shops, or served at restaurants like the French Laundry on *amuse-bouches*.

Presented on a crostini baked with olive oil and rubbed with garlic, Délice is a perfect starter. Scooped on strawberries and drizzled with honey and balsamic vinegar or used in place of custard on a fresh fruit tart, Délice makes people happy to see cheese on the dessert plate. And remember—just like a toddler in a tiara, triple crèmes love sparkles. Proseccos, Cavas, Champagnes, and Cremants, and when things get a little sweeter at the end of the night, think Moscato d'Asti.

Other fromage blancs (made only from cow's milk) are Dairy Goddess's from Lemoore, California (available online outside California); Bellwether's from Sonoma, California; and Vermont Butter & Cheese Creamery's from Websterville, Vermont (both are distributed nationwide).

Nettle Meadow Kunik, New York

Some serious cheese folk turn their nose up at triple crèmes. They're treated like the beautiful sister who, unlike her less-attractive sibling with a Harvard doctorate in sixteenth-century English literature, her parents trust will always be able to find employment, despite her lack of job skills and average education level.

And just like Suzie, the smiling, beautiful sibling, triples are more often than not, not taken seriously. They're seen as fluff—too delicious to deserve critical contemplation.

That's why Nettle Meadow Kunik, a dynamic mixed-milk triple, is a blessing in disguise for serious or elitist cheese lovers everywhere. Allowing the connoisseur to indulge in the decadence of a creamy cheese without feeling like they're turning their back on intelligent, complex wheels, Kunik intellectualizes the genre.

Thank a goat and a cow for that.

Kunik is made in Thurman, New York, with 75 percent goat's milk from the Nettle Meadow's herd of Nigerian dwarves and Nubian–La Mancha crosses, and 25 percent Jersey cow cream from neighboring farms in western Massachusetts. The goat's milk is already especially rich because of the breed mix. When they add extra-butterfat Jersey cream to the mix, the creaminess can't be stopped.

Wrapped in a bloomy white rind, Kunik comes in various wheel sizes from cute and tiny to cheesecake-sized, all delicious. The goat's milk offers liveliness to a style that can fall a little flat at times if not done right. Nettle Meadow's herd is allowed to graze on wild grasses, nettles, and herbs at the farm. The combo of the flavor that grazing provides and the naturally lively and lemony taste of goat's milk makes for an animated base highlighted by cream. The end result tastes like fresh hazelnuts mixed with cream, butter, a fresh herb or two, and drizzled with just-squeezed lemon juice.

To make Kunik, cheesemakers Lorraine Lambiase and Sheila Flanagan start out with pasteurized goat's milk, to which they add cream. As with nearly all other bloomy-rinded cheeses, cultures and the *Penicillium candidum* mold that initiates the white, Brie-like rind are added to the milk. Then the rennet goes in and the curds are left to set, then later cut, ladled into forms, brined, and refrigerated until sold.

One of the biggest challenges with such creamy cheeses, according to Flanagan, is that the curd varies throughout the season depending on the animal's diet, its lactation cycle, and the weather. When the curd is moister (as it often is in the summer, when there is more water in the milk), it's harder to set, and the amount of culture and rennet added must be adjusted so the curd won't break after the wheel is already formed and aging.

"It's kind of the artsy side of cheesemaking—even the three batches of Kunik we make every day will taste a little different. It's a challenge, but it keeps it interesting."

Lambiase and Flanagan don't shy away from a challenge. They were taken with the original Kunik when they bought Nettle Meadow in 2005, but thought the cheese could be even better and more consistent.

In addition to the curd being so variable because of moisture fluctuation, a triple crème's being is easily threatened by changing temperatures and climate. Because their aging room, an antiquated butter cellar and old cow barn, was so temperature sensitive, before the current team bought Nettle Meadow, Kunik would get to shops in varying states. Sometimes it was picture perfect, other times it leeched water because it got too wet in the cellar, and still other times it had a cracked rind because the cellar was too dry. The Nettle Meadow team has since installed air-conditioning and humidity controls, but says Flanigan, "we still check humidity and temperature minute by minute."

These seemingly simple cheeses are really more complex to make than the average cheese snob realizes. One doesn't have to write them off for just being pretty and walking through life with a silver spoon in their mouth. They've overcome challenges to get as yummy as they are.

Triples are, hands down, the best bubbly pairing ever. Nearly any bubbly from a rosé Cava to a Champagne to Crémant de Loire loves a triple. And because this is a mixed milk, it can handle a little more depth in a wine. Think of all the things you can pair with a goat cheese from a Sauvignon Blanc from Sancerre to a high-acidity red such as Cabernet Franc or Dolcetto. Richer whites such as oaked Chardonnays and Viogniers work, too, because they match the triple's buttery flavors.

A couple other double and triple mixed milks to try are Vermont Butter & Cheese Creamery's Crémont from Websterville, Vermont (goat and cow); Nancy's Camembert from Old Chatham, New York (sheep and cow); and Mélange by Andante Dairy in Sonoma, California (goat and cow). All but Andante should be relatively easy to find.

Délice de la Vallée Fromage Blanc Sausage Phyllo Triangles

MAKES 20–25 TRIANGLES

These cheese, dried fruit, and sausage hors d'oeuvre triangles are addictively salty-sweet. The soft, fluffy, lightly grainy Délice de la Vallée works wonders when warmed, and the phyllo adds a nice crunch. If Délice isn't available near you, use another fromage blanc, ricotta, or chèvre. Just be sure to drain the cheese if it is very wet.

2 tablespoons untoasted pine nuts
1 bratwurst, removed from casing
2 cups firmly packed baby spinach
2 tablespoons dried currants
¼ cup golden raisins
8 ounces Délice de la Vallée
⅛ teaspoon salt
1 cube butter, melted and kept warm
1 box phyllo dough

Preheat oven to 375 degrees.

Toast the pine nuts over medium-low heat in a small-sized sauté pan for 5–10 minutes, shaking the pan to brown evenly. Put in a medium-sized bowl. Bring the same small-sized sauté pan to medium heat. Add the sausage meat to the pan and cook for 5–10 minutes, until browned. Add to the pine nut bowl and cool.

Bring a small pot of salted water to a boil. Add the spinach, blanching it for only 20 seconds. Drain into a colander and rinse immediately under cold water. Wring all the water from the spinach by squeezing it in a clean cloth towel or napkin. Put the spinach into the same bowl that the sausage and pine nuts are in, breaking up the spinach while adding it to the bowl. Add the currants, raisins, cheese, and salt.

Have a moist towel and the warm butter handy for the phyllo. Make sure you have a large clean, dry counter space to begin your work. Unroll the phyllo, move it to the side, and cover the stack with the towel. You'll be working with one sheet at a time and covering the big stack after removing each sheet.

Bring one phyllo sheet directly in front of you and place horizontally. Brush lightly with melted butter. Repeat with two more sheets, making a buttered stack three sheets high. Cut this stack up and down into eight vertical strips. These strips will be folded into filled phyllo triangles one at a time.

Place a heaping teaspoon of the filling you just prepared on the bottom of the strip. Working with one strip at a time, fold the right-hand corner of the strip up and across to the left so that an edge of a triangle starts to form out of the bottom-right-hand corner. Now fold the triangle up. Next, take the triangle that's been formed and flip to the right. Don't worry if the filling comes out the corners at first because by the time you've finished forming the triangle, the filling will be contained. Repeat the phyllo process until the entire strip is wrapped around the filling. Rewrap and refreeze any remaining phyllo. Brush the tops of the triangles with melted butter. Cook the triangles for 10–12 minutes or until wrapping is golden brown and crispy. Let cool 5 minutes before serving.

Leaf Wrapped

• • • • •

Flavored, Preserved, and *Lord of the Rings* Ready

There's a scene in *The Return of the King* before Frodo almost gets eaten by a spider the size of three stacked unicorns when he accuses Sam of stealing his last piece of lembas bread. Of course, Sam didn't steal the cheese; it was shifty Gollum setting him up, but this scene perfectly sets the story for leaf-wrapped cheeses. Like the lembas, the cheeses of topic are also wrapped in leaves from their respective shires.

Back in hobbit and more recent human times, wrapping food in leaves was like sticking a sandwich in a plastic baggie. It was a mode of transport. Since cheese is a nourishing, high-energy food, it was a good choice for those on the move, and it needed protection on its trips. Cheesemakers would wrap up wheels before their journey or sometimes as quickly as after salting in the make area.

Now, leaves serve as pliable rinds in the aging room. Sometimes cheesemakers don't want their softer cheeses to acquire a thick, hard rind but still desire something to protect it from outside forces. After being blanched or soaked in alcohol, leaves are the perfect barrier for softer cheeses.

Selecting leaves and/or alcohols from the region where they make their cheese has become a source of pride for cheesemakers. Sure there's the occasional homage to a European cheese that uses a shipped leaf or two, but most cheesemakers use wrappers to say something about their community. Wine-growing areas use grape leaves to honor the practice. Cheesemakers proud of their state's moonshine and corn might use husks to wrap and whiskey to soak. Rind protection aside, some cheesemakers just put their cheeses in leaves because it tastes good. Did we already mention pear brandy?

Wrapping cheese in leaves has become more than just a way to keep shepherds and hobbits from starving before they get to Mordor. It's become a way for cheesemakers to put their area's or inspiration's stamp on their cheese, whether the stamp is indicative of the region's boundary-crossing culinary connections with Mexico as with the hoja santa leaf, or whether it links it to inventive Southern bootleggers with moonshine and corn husks.

Mozzarella Company Hoja Santa, Texas

Hoja Santa is the style of cheese that Frodo Baggins's and Sam Gamgee's mothers would have packed the boys if they left for their ring trip from Mesoamerica instead of Middle-earth. The leaves would have kept the cheese moist, and would have provided that taste of home that apprehensive hobbits need when venturing from the Mesoamerican shire for the first time.

Wrapped in hoja santa leaves, Hoja Santa is a cheese that's all Texas. Paula Lambert of Mozzarella Company in Dallas has been crafting this fresh goat cheese bundle for around fifteen years.

Standing an inch high and about the diameter of a coffee mug, Hoja Santa is a proud local little cheese that resembles the French leaf-wrapped cheese Banon. Its rind is made up of dark green hoja santa leaves that have been blanched before wrapping. The leaves stay wet after they're blanched and once they're packaged, so if hobbits wanted to eat the leaves along with the fresh cheese inside (totally doable), wrapping it with an additional fresh leaf would have been advisable.

Unwrapping the leaves exposes a bright white interior and a taste that will surprise anyone expecting a chèvre-like experience. All flavors imparted by the hoja santa leaf, the cheese tastes like . . . fresh cheese magic. The hoja santa leaf, native to Mesoamerica (which, *claro que si*, used to include Texas) is rich with safriole oil—the oil that gives sassafras its sassafras-iness. The safriole and the mint, lemony flavors provided from the hoja santa leaf, bring out the goat's milk's already naturally lively flavors. It's a perfect wrapper.

Lambert, a smiling woman with a Southern accent so homey and sweet that it makes you forget the entrepreneur runs one of the most successful artisan cheese companies in the United States, says she started to realize hoja santa's potential after trying dishes chefs created featuring the leaf in Dallas and Mexico City. It's traditionally used in Latino and Latin American cultures to wrap tamales, chicken, and fish, and in Mexico's *mole verde*. Lambert took a liking to the leaf's flavors and decided she wanted to make her version of France's Banon, Texas-style. Excited to use a leaf that is indigenous to the area and that reflects the state's culture, Lambert buys the leaves from local herb growers, some of whom she's contracted with specifically to grow the herb.

Before the leaves do their thing, Lambert starts out with pasteurized milk when making hoja. Cultures and rennet are added, then the milk is ladled into molds by hand to keep the curds from breaking and drained overnight. In the morning, the cheese is unmolded and salted. Then it is turned every day for a week. After those seven days, the cheese is wrapped in the blanched leaves (Lambert's cheesemakers blanch/dunk the leaves in boiling water on-site and don't use alcohol for flavor as many do), vacuum-sealed in plastic, and left to marinate. It could go straight to the shops after a week or two, or it could age for up to six months. When younger, it's less potent. After six months, it becomes dense and creamier, and the leaf's flavors pop even more.

Flavors of sassafras and mint make the cheese cry for a simple alcohol pairing that won't be put out if Hoja Santa steals the lime-light. Lambert prefers lighter beers, white wines, or Champagnes. I second her pairing suggestion and will say nearly any sparkling from Cava to Champagne would do the trick, and that any white wines served should be void of oak, except the occasional Champagne. Mint, sassafras, and oak = not delicious. Red wines should be avoided alto-gether unless they have amazingly light oak or are traditionally herbal such as Cabernet Franc or Mencia. Do try Hoja Santa with a Mesoamerican beverage that doesn't sit in a barrel, such as tequila plata. If you like a little burn with your booze, try it with moonshine.

Hoja Santa is flavorful enough on its own, at room temperature, but is also good heated. If Lambert's not having hers on a cracker (her base of choice), she often just pops it in a 350-degree oven for five minutes. When it's warm, the center oozes like a molten cake.

Other leaf-wrapped young cheeses to try are Capriole's O'Banon (goat cheese wrapped in chestnut leaves soaked in bourbon, widely available) from Greenville, Indiana; Love Tree's Little Holmes (goat cheese sprinkled with peppermint then wrapped in nettles, rare) from Grantsburg, Wisconsin; and the Saxelby Cheese–Seal Cove collabora-tion, Sozzled Pearl (goat's and cow's milks wrapped in bourbon-soaked grape leaves) from Lamoine, Maine.

Rogue River Blue, Oregon

Once a summer, about fifteen Rogue River Blue pilgrims crawl out of their beds before the first jaybird chirps. After chugging liters of coffee and lathering more sunscreen than Tammy Faye Bakker layered mascara, they head to Carpenter Hill Vineyards to pick garbage bags full of specifically shaped Syrah leaves. Before 5:30 a.m. For six or more hours. In the sun. For free (or for a lovely catered lunch).

This is the sort of blind devotion Rogue River Blue demands from its followers. Wrapped in grape leaves soaked in Oregon-made pear brandy, Rogue River Blue is an aged *Penicillium roqueforti*–based cheese that looks like Spain's leaf-and-raffia-wrapped Valdéon. Draped

Rogue River Blue

with a dark, soft leaf, the paste is flecked with mold that grows vibrantly blue and golden toward the center.

Brown butter, hazelnuts, autumn truffles, vanilla, chocolate, Himalayan blackberry, and bacon. Soft-spoken Rogue co-owner David Gremmels describes the flavors in his cheese with the passion of a classical music lover extolling his favorite piece. Though an entire wedge of Rogue calls to a blue cheese lover, one can't help going straight for the creamy core that's flecked with occasional amino acid and calcium crystals. And then, of course, go back for a sample of the meaty exterior.

In 2001, owners David Gremmels and Cary Bryant knew they had to start protecting the delicate rind of Rogue River Blue. But with what? Because Rogue wanted to further the company's mission of contributing to the community's sustainability through cheese, they decided to stay local and go green. Gremmels called Carpenter Hill, a vineyard that helped to make a name for Southern Oregon's Rogue River Valley, and asked if he could come get a couple thousand leaves.

"You don't know how strange the request was, eight years ago," says Lee Mankin, Carpenter Hill Vineyard owner, shaking his head. "David calls me up and says he wants fifty thousand leaves. I ask myself, are you kidding me? And he's willing to come and pick them himself?"

It was the perfect pairing. For Mankin, it's proactive pruning—he calls Rogue around the time he'd have to get rid of the leaves in order for the grapes to get enough sun anyhow. And Gremmels and his team of mainly volunteers get to pick leaves in a vineyard that offers one of the prettiest views of Southern Oregon.

After the leaves are picked in June or July when the grapes are just starting to form, Rogue soaks the leaves in pear brandy made with Rogue River Valley pears for a year to purify them. Then they wrap the eight-month-plus-old blue wheels, which up to this point are made in a similar fashion to most blues except with extremely rich, fall unpasteurized "equinox milk," with six to seven leaves. The cheese is released anywhere from four months to a year later, when the combination of the butterfat from the seasonal milk and the leaves' tannins and pear flavors impart a silky, balanced texture and subtle fruity and meaty flavors.

Rogue is what Gremmels calls a third-generation blue. Prior to Rogue, the main blue style in the United States was Danish. When Tom Vella, Sonoma cheesemaker, visited Roquefort in the 1950s and opened Rogue in Oregon, he introduced the French blue cheese style at home. Later, his cheesemaker son Ignacio (better known as Ig) made Rogue's Oregonzola to honor his father's life. Rogue River Blue is the third blue to come out of Rogue, no longer owned by Vella, but as Gremmels states it, always made in part to honor the immeasurably influential Ig Vella, one of Gremmel's cheese mentors.

I haven't been able to find many North American leaf-wrapped blues, but have no doubt there are some under-the-radar versions to be found, and more on the way, after the success of Rogue River.

Bonnyclabber Moonshine, Virginia

Cheesemaker Rona Sullivan is a woman on a mission. An advocate of Southern cheese history, culture, and old methods, Rona has a passion for her region, and this led her to study the South's cheeseways when others looked north (or west, or east). After seeking out obscure manuscripts and journals dating back to the seventeenth century to fill in local cheese history blanks, Sullivan decided to focus on clabbered-milk cheese—a style of acid-set culturing typical of seventeenth-century Virginia, but rarely seen or referenced any longer in the United States. Until Moonshine.

Bonnyclabber Moonshine is one of the most regionally inspired cheeses one can find. From the foot of Wake, Virginia's Blue Ridge Mountains, Bonnyclabber Moonshine is wrapped with local corn husks that have been soaked in Virginia's own Belmont Farm's Virginia Lightning moonshine. It's made without rennet or cultures in a style so traditional to the area that when Irish-Scots passed through the mountainous region in the 1800s and saw locals eating clabbered cream and bread or porridge, just like they did back home, they christened it "Bonnyclabber country."

Once packaged, Moonshine looks like a square tamale, or an Italian leaf-wrapped robiola (sometimes Moonshine comes in a rectangular shape; sometimes it's more round). The taste, which one might think would be slightly jarring because of the famed moonshine kick, is gentle. Because customers prefer lighter flavors, cheesemaker Sullivan pasteurizes Moonshine (most of her other cheeses are made from raw milk) so she doesn't have to age it past sixty days and can preserve the cheese's subtleties. Its flavors are sweet, milky, lemony, what some might call "farmhousey," with a slight moonshine kick reminiscent of corn, cooked straight on a fire.

To make Moonshine, Sullivan starts out by clabbering goat's milk. "Clabbering" is allowing lactic acid to naturally develop in milk by letting it sit in an area with a temperature of eighty to one hundred degrees for twenty-four to forty-eight hours so that it naturally starts to curdle and coagulate without any help from cheese cultures or rennet. The aforementioned Loire Valley–inspired cheesemakers let their soft-ripened cheese start to coagulatate via this lactic acid method, too, but most also use rennet, which isn't traditional when just clabbering. Because Sullivan uses pasteurized milk, which lacks the ability to self-clabber, she kickstarts the clabbering process by adding a little yogurt to the milk. Then she leaves it alone for a day.

"It's great, it allows me to multitask, which of course was an appeal in the old days," says Sullivan. "I can go up to the house and make things from scratch like my grandmother would while the cheese is clabbering in the cheese room."

Although an old European method, clabbering fell out of fashion here when cheese became industrial. Since it took longer to clabber than just add rennet or cultures, and required intense attention to temperatures and climate for the coagulation to start indigenously, commercial cheesemakers had little interest in the process. After the industrial revolution, the focus was on production, and slow methods fell by the wayside.

Those who continued clabbering, like some in the Virginia hills, did it only for themselves. As Sullivan puts it, those who made cheese and wrote at the time, wrote about rennet, and most made cheese in larger scale. The ones who clabbered were too busy on their farmstead, logging, mining, etc., to write about the process, and pretty soon, according to Sullivan, people started thinking of clabbering as a "backwoods," "slow process." At that time, that meant outdated and counterproductive. Now, it means it's a heritage method, slow-food style. Sullivan started clabbering her cheese to sell in 1999.

As many did before her, Sullivan starts out by putting fresh milk in vessels to clabber in a warm room. In her case, it's two-and-a-half-gallon covered jars. One or two days later, once the curd has firmed so it "jiggles and splits like Jell-O," says the cheesemaker, she drains the curd in a tightly woven butter muslin cloth by hanging it for twenty-four hours. Then, she lightly salts the curd and dries it in the refrigerator for several days. Once the cheese starts to peel away from the cloth, she puts Moonshine in molds and flips them several times. Then she portions them, salts the rinds, and wraps them in liquor-soaked corn husks. Then, to the shop—they're sold within a week or two.

After Moonshine hits the shop, it can be enjoyed in a multitude of ways. I like it plain, served on a crostini or nut cracker, maybe with a little honey if the moonshine kicks in strong (which it rarely does). I also like it warmed. Moonshine can be tossed on a grill, as the husks can take direct heat, then spooned straight from the husk onto crusty bread or an apple slice. I keep the booze pairing simple—Sauvignon Blanc, with beers, or if you dare, moonshine. If you do dare, may the cheese forces be with you, and the shots be small. This is still a developing cheese category, so there aren't many to be found, but Bonnyclabber also makes another corn-husk-wrapped cheese called Sandybotttom—a pepper-encrusted goat cheese.

Hoja Santa Frisée and Persimmon Chèvre Chaud with Sweet, Spiced Nuts

SERVES 4

This fall-weather salad is my take on chèvre chaud. I made it with Hoja Santa in mind, but other leaf-wrapped goat cheeses would work, too. Here, the hoja santa leaf and the tarragon flavors meld expertly, as do the spicy persimmon and spices in the candied walnuts and pumpkin seeds. This salad offers comfort and warmth in colder months especially.

1½ cups walnuts
½ cup shelled pumpkin seeds
1 egg white, lightly beaten
5 tablespoons brown sugar
¼ teaspoon cinnamon
½ teaspoon salt
⅛ teaspoon powdered chili pepper
¼ teaspoon cocoa powder
1 tablespoon shallots, finely chopped
½ tablespoon tarragon, finely chopped
1 tablespoon balsamic vinegar
3 tablespoons extra virgin olive oil
¼ teaspoon salt
2 medium Fuyu or other firm-style persimmons
2 Hoja Santa cheeses
1 head radicchio, cleaned and trimmed into bite-size pieces
1 head frisée, cleaned and trimmed into bite-size pieces
salt and pepper to taste

Preheat oven to 350 degrees.
   Put walnuts, pumpkin seeds, egg white, sugar, spices, and ½ teaspoon salt in a medium-sized bowl and mix well to coat all

nuts and seeds. Spread over a silicon sheet or buttered piece of parchment paper. Bake for 15 minutes, or until nuts are crunchy and no longer wet. Set aside to cool.

Whisk shallots, tarragon, vinegar, olive oil, and ¼ salt together in a small bowl for your vinaigrette.

Cut persimmons into thin slices.

Put both pieces of Hoja Santa in the oven. Bake for 10 minutes, or until center becomes soft and molten (test by feel).

While the cheese is baking, mix raddichio, frisée, persimmon, and vinaigrette together in a large bowl. Season with salt and pepper to taste. Divide onto four salad plates. Sprinkle candied nuts over the salad (you will have extra). Once Hoja Santa is ready, cut in half and place each half on top of the lettuces. Serve.

American Originals and Inspirations

• • • • •

Room to Grow

This is a motley category. It contains two modern cheeses that don't fit neatly into this book's specific genres and a fabled one whose heyday was before Prohibition that nearly transcends another category. Behind the scenes, it offers a home to many other square peg artisan cheeses that also do not fit into round holes.

The time of these cheeses is coming (or will come again). At this moment, I can see where the two salient styles could be slipped in another category with some explanation. For example, Bardwell's Pawlet could be added to the washed rind or Alpine sections, because it is indeed both washed and inspired by Northern Italy. However, as I write, more people are creating similar cheeses that could help build Pawlet and its cousins their own category, likely for Northern Italian cheeses, or . . . who knows.

We have to wait to see what happens. Drawing preemptive boundaries on cheese styles during their development years is like forcing a five-year-old to stay within the lines of his coloring book. It's stifling, and makes us look fussy in front of others who are watching.

Then there's Limburger. A cheese as storied as Superman, as etched in American history as apple pie, and as linked to a time and place as *Mad Men*'s Don Draper, I couldn't in good conscience just slip it in with the other washed rinds. Though its popularity has fluctuated since its inception and now only one cheese plant produces all the Limburger made in this country, it's a legend, an inspiration, and quite frankly, too different in taste and history from the other washeds to just be dropped in.

Widmer's Brick cheese from Wisconsin, which is both an American original and nearly as storied as Limburger, could find a happy home in this category, as could the rare small batch Monterey Jacks or artisanal Provolone styles. This genre serves as a harbor, for some maybe a permanent one, but for most, just a place to stop and have a cup of coffee and maybe a piece of pie on their leisurely drive through town. It's open to further definition and reclassification, and cheeses may leave to create their own lives and families whenever cheesemakers wish, because nobody puts these babies in the corner.

Consider Bardwell Farm Pawlet, Vermont

What happens when a top food literary agent and her architect husband decide they want to make cheese in Vermont? They leave their home in New York City for a piece of land idyllic enough to make the entire French countryside jealous, open a café, buy goats, hire a master cheesemaker, and start pumping out wheels that make it in no time to the cheese menu at Manhattan's three-Michelin-starred restaurant Per Se.

Consider Bardwell Farms in West Pawlet, Vermont, which so closely borders New York State that I accidentally crossed state lines twice when visiting, is known for their award-winning goat cheese wheels. One of their most outstanding, lovable cheeses, however, is their cow's milk Pawlet.

Pawlet is a semisoft, orange-rinded Jersey milk cheese that owner Angela Miller says helps form family cheese bridges. While it's mild enough that kids will down it by the slice after school, it is sophisticated enough to interest parents who would like to sit down and share cheese with their children.

It has a smooth paste with a similar texture to a young asiago that makes it a great melting cheese—time to get rid of that rubbery "mozzarella" on pizza pies. In its youngest state, Pawlet is a gentle cheese that tastes like butter and cream. As it ages, its washed rind (see "Washed and Smeared Rinds" on page 165 to learn more) demands more attention, and Pawlet develops a slight tang and a scent that starts to suggest a dash of *Époisses* or *Tallegio* funk.

Made in the style of Northern Italian semisoft washed rinds, Pawlet is inspired by the mountain cheeses of Piedmont. When the owners and cheesemakers decided they wanted to make a cow's milk cheese to sell during the season when their goats weren't milking because they were breeding, they looked toward what Miller calls the "peasant cheese" style sold in Piedmont's farmer's markets.

To make Pawlet, the cheesemakers start with their neighbor's Jersey cow's milk. (Consider Bardwell always aims to use just their own or their neighbor's milk to support their local dairies.) Then they add the secret blend of cultures of rennet to the unpasteurized milk to get the curds coagulating.

As is typical of the style, the cheesemakers cut the curds to what they call "medium size"—to create a cheese with less moisture than a Camembert, but more moisture than a cheddar. After cooking the curds briefly, they scoop them into molds and press them under plastic jugs filled with sand for about two hours or until, as one Consider

Bardwell cheesemaker says, "they look right." Next, they're brined with saltwater, then allowed to dry out. Then, to the cheese caves, where the rinds are rubbed down or "washed" with saltwater to encourage the *Brevibacterious linens* that make a washed rind so special for three to four months.

Its production is what makes Pawlet such a spectacular melting cheese. By keeping the curds large and the aging time under six months, the cheesemakers inspire a semisoft yet creamy paste. Sure, it's good on its own and has the power to charm little kids who are still on "yellow" or "white" cheese terms, but its main thrilling point beyond the cheese plate is how well it gets gooey between two pieces of buttered bread. When warmed, it becomes shiny, it never breaks off into chunks, and the flavors from the washed rind help to keep the whole grilled cheese thing compelling. Owner Angela Miller knows this. The pressed sandwiches she serves in her Consider Bardwell Farm Cafe (open on weekends only) alongside her baked goods could win people over to the Pawlet side.

When serving cheese plate style, serve Pawlet with a condiment that has a little punch or sweetness, such as fig jam or chutney (although these are also good spread on grilled cheese). If sipping with wine, serve with a dry or slightly sweet Riesling or Gewürztraminer.

The same suggestions go for somewhat similar cheeses also inspired by Northen Italian cheesemaking practices, such as Cowgirl Creamery's Wagon Wheel from Point Reyes, California (created in part so San Francisco's Zuni Café would have a good local pizza melter); Nicasio's Toma Alta from Sonoma, California; or the related, but much more raclette-styled cheeses such as Sequatchie Cove Farm's Coppinger from Sequatchie, Tennessee, and Spring Brook's Reading from Reading, Vermont (both a little harder to find nationally).

Chalet Cheese Cooperative Limburger, Wisconsin

Mighty Mouse, the crime-solving mouse enrobed in cape and body suit, has only one downfall. Limburger. Whether he's about to save a child from an infamous assassin or is in the middle of a covert operation to catch a chipmunk bandit, if he smells Limburger, Mighty is as good as gone. While the smear-ripened delight can put a smile on a Limburger fan's face like that on a stoner's visiting Humboldt during harvest, Mighty cowers under the cheese's intensity.

Once considered an everyday cheese by many Americans, Limburger is now mainly portrayed in the media as a stinky, distracting intrusion. That is, if it is portrayed at all. Demand for this cheese has dropped since its heyday. Formerly made all over the Midwest, Limburger is now produced by only one company in the country—Chalet Cheese Cooperative, the oldest operating farmer co-op in Monroe, Wisconsin. Despite its shifting popularity, head Chalet cheesemaker Myron Olson doesn't worry about his plant's closure.

"The typical consumer may be seventy-eight years old," says Olson, "but they'll swim a river and climb a mountain to get their Limburger."

If the carfuls of people from neighboring states making the pilgrimage to see how this little orange block is made mean something, Olson is right. A rectangular cheese, most blocks of Limburger are half a pound. Underneath their foil wrapping they are bright orange with a French vanilla ice cream–colored center.

Limburger isn't always as strong as the ones that have offended the inappropriately named cartoon mouse. A young block of it is a completely different animal from an aged one. Some who've tried an older, stronger version and decided they hate the cheese might have fallen in love with a less mature one paired with a little strawberry jam (Olson's favorite pairing).

Chalet puts a guide on the wrapper to assist the Limburger-curious. The washed rind novice would likely love the cheese when a month old. Then, it's sweet, buttery, gentle, with a just enough of a washed rind flavor to keep it interesting. At two-and-a-half months, the *Brevibacterium linens* (the bacteria responsible for making washed rinds orange and funky) have started to break down the cheese so it's softer and more spreadable, and it develops the characteristics that made Limburger famous—a slightly stinky sock scent and sweet, robust flavors that beg to be paired with a thick slice of rye bread, mustard, jam, or beer.

Limburger started out slathered on bread in this country. Working-class cheese-loving European immigrants who ate the cheese around the Limburg area (formerly part of Germany, the Netherlands, and Belgium) came to Midwestern hubs such as Monroe and started making their own in the late 1800s. They cut thick slices of Limburger, spread it on rye bread slathered with brown mustard, topped it with onion slices, and served it with beer. Back then many immigrants even considered Limburger a health food. Believing its particular bacteria flora helped with digestion, they piled it atop bread lavishly. It wasn't until Prohibition times that its popularity started to wane, Olson reports.

Limburger was part of the pub culture, and when workers couldn't have their Limburger sandwiches washed down with beer on their lunch break, they ate a lot less of the beauty. Sales went down, and after Prohibition the robust flavor of the cheese now seemed too strong for many. Some also turned their backs on favorite foods from their home country such as Limburger in attempt to acclimate better to their new home. Others, caught up in America's journey into the pristine and sanitized era of food where processed and tidy were considered better, lost interest in the cheese.

Unlike many large-scale German interpretations of the cheese, American Limburger made in the United States is just as artisanal now as it was when it was the belle of the pub party. After Olson and his team get the party going by adding cultures and rennet to the pasteurized milk and cut the curd large, they pour the curds into large rectangular molds. The rectangular molds get flipped, then sit overnight. The next morning the large blocks are cut into smaller blocks, salted, then wet down with salt water twice a day for a week. A week later they're inoculated. They're washed down twice with the original Chalet wash with all the original delicious flora from 1911 so their rinds become sticky and tacky, and a week later they're wrapped in custom foil that allows the cheese to breathe. Then they're sent to the cooler, where the *B. linens* bacteria activate.

As back in Limburger's good ole days, I like Limburger with beer. Powerful Belgian beer. As it gets older, it craves a sweeter one like a Belgian tripel. As for wines, I like it with a sweet Riesling, Gewürztraminer, or dessert white wine such as a late-harvest Viognier, Chenin Blanc, or Sauvignon Blanc. While I'd ideally choose a more local jam producer, darn, that jar of Smucker's strawberry preserves sitting on the Chalet sample table tasted good with the washed rind. It makes me think that Limburger, honey, and fresh strawberries would make a mighty fine dessert.

Limburger is an inspiration to nearly all American washed rinds around—the closest you'll find to Limburger is . . . Limburger. Or maybe Liederkranz, also made by Chalet Cheese.

Bleating Heart Sonoma Toma, California

Seana Doughty rocks her 125-square-foot aging room in Sonoma the way Pat Benatar would a sold-out concert in a tiny venue in the eighties—with the skill of a trained and passionate artist determined to perform despite obstacles, and with a fair amount of lip gloss.

Her cheeses don't hold back either. Some are stamped with hearts on their rinds. Others have indented rinds that look like someone's been using them as a squishy toy. Others, confidently flaunting a curvaceous figure, hit the town with names such as Fat Bottom Girl.

Bleating Heart and its cheeses such as Sonoma Toma are one-of-a-kind American originals. They demonstrate American motivation and innovations in contemporary cheesemaking and show how modern cheeses are shaped by their surrounding environment.

A cow's milk wheel with a soft brownish-gray mold on its rustic rind, Sonoma Toma is a semisoft cylinder that reaches about two pounds. It has a light basket weave pattern, its rind is dotted with

Sonoma Toma

fingerprint indentations, and it leans a little to the right. Or left, depending on which way the wind is blowing.

With tastes of fresh cream, buttermilk, salted butter, and an earthy lemony finish, the Toma is aged from three to four months. With a plum or apricot compote and a toasted nut or two, it makes a great cheese course. When heated, it melts into a lively cream that takes soft scrambled eggs to a happy place.

Sonoma Toma was cheesemaker Seana Doughty's experiment wheel. Inspired by the cheeses in France whose rind formation is left up to the ambient molds of the region, Doughty wanted to see what would happen if she left a wheel to its own devices. So she decided not to add molds to the batch of milk at the beginning of the cheese-making process. Then, like a good parent, she gave her child a solid upbringing—good milk, lots of hugs and attention, proper ventilation—and watched to see what developed.

The breezes and natural humidity flowing through the small Sonoma wine country town and the apple orchard outside Doughty's tiny make room lent their own molds to the wheel. The firm rind is a smooth dusty light gray, brown, and white hue that lightly gives to the touch and whose flavors add an earthiness to the cheese. Unadulterated by additions that would inspire a Brie-like rind or holes like those in an Emmenthaler, the Sonoma Toma's rind was as shaped by the surrounding environment as is the Bleating Heart Enterprise.

Sonoma Toma wasn't cheesemaker Seana Doughty's dream wheel. Doughty started Bleating Heart in 2009 with the intention of focusing entirely on sheep's milk cheeses, but quickly learned that securing enough sheep's milk in California was harder than parking at a farmer's market in Berkeley without being cut off by a car sporting a peace sticker.

So Doughty headed to Wisconsin in the dead of winter with a truck to gather a flock of twelve sheep. Then she partnered with a neighboring creamery that cares for and milks her sheep when Doughty doesn't have time, leased space to make cheese in a local creamery, and built an affinage room outside her family home because she has neither the space nor the money to invest in land or a farm in wine country. Then, when her sheep weren't producing enough milk to satisfy her cheesemaking cravings, she started buying goat's and cow's milk, too.

Doughty exemplifies an up-and-coming breed of modern American cheesemakers—those whose passion drives them to create spaces for themselves in environments where before only those with family land or wealth had the ability.

And her cheeses, which show a mix of creativity and relenting to natural forces at work—be they financial, spatial, or moldy—are a perfect example of an American Original.

Two other natural-rinded cheeses that may or may not claim any regional inspiration are Kenswick Creamery Wallaby from Newburg, Pennsylvania; and Consider Bardwell's Equinox from West Pawlet, Vermont.

Sonoma Toma Yuba Mushroom Blintzes

MAKES 4–6 BLINTZES

My chef fromager friend Tia Keenan inspired these yuba blintzes when I saw her work her magic on yuba sheets. Yuba sheets are essentially tofu skins. They're soft, flexible, and skimmed from the top of the tofu pot when making tofu. In this recipe, the tofu skin's sweet, earthy flavors play off like flavors in Sonoma Toma, and the mushrooms add extra oomph. If you can find yuba, definitely use yuba; if you can't find it, make blintzes from a traditional blintz recipe. Any earthy semisoft, natural rind cheese will work in this blintz, as would not-too-pungent washed rind (just slice, not grate, if soft). Serve this with a side salad for a great brunch.

8 ounces portabello mushrooms, or approximately
    2 caps, thinly sliced
8 ounces oyster mushrooms, trimmed and sliced if
    large
1–3 tablespoons butter
1 medium shallot, finely chopped
5 ounces grated Sonoma Toma
½ teaspoon fresh lemon juice
salt and pepper to taste
3–6 yuba sheets, cut into 4–6 four-inch squares
1½ tablespoons butter

Combine the mushrooms.
    Bring a large sauté pan to medium-high heat. Add ½ tablespoon butter, melted. Add half of the mushrooms. Sear for 2 minutes, or until the mushrooms have taken on a bit of color, then reduce heat to medium and cook the mushrooms for 7 minutes more, flipping occasionally. Add half of the shallots to the mushrooms, stir, and cook for 2 more minutes. Transfer to a medium-sized bowl. Repeat with the second batch of mushrooms. Let cool. Once cool, drain the moisture from the mush-

rooms (you can save this liquid for a "pasta" sauce and cook with any remaining yuba strips later if you wish).

Add cheese and lemon juice to the mushroom bowl and mix well. Salt and pepper to taste.

Lay out all of the four-inch yuba squares on your work surface. Center, as best you can, one-fifth of the mushroom filling in the middle of the square. If the yuba breaks, use scraps left from cutting the squares to patch it. Fold sides toward the center one at a time. Repeat with each yuba square until all are prepared as directed.

Heat a large sauté pan to medium heat. Add the butter (use half of the butter if you need to work in batches to brown all the blintzes). Gently place the blintzes in the pan with a spatula. After the yuba turns golden brown, flip the blintzes, then lower the heat to low. Cook for 5 more minutes on each side or until the cheese is melted and the filling is hot. Serve while hot.

Alpine Influence

•   •   •   •   •

Good Grass, Genes, and Breeding

The Alps are known for snowy peaks, wildflowers, and ginormous wheels of cheese such as Gruyère, Comté, Beaufort, and Raclette, which build impressive muscles in people who flip them for a living. Aside from being made around the hills that are dear to Heidi's heart, Alpine wheels have other defining characteristics that make them stand out in a crowd, both back home and here.

In the Alps, the wheels are large. Cheesemakers would traditionally make large wheels in part because it was easier to take fewer trips up and down the hills with fewer cheeses. There were only one or two guys making cheese in a hut on the top of the mountain. Since this isn't so much of a concern in the United States, many artisan wheels have shrunk to eight pounds or so. There is also a small Alpine cheese subculture comprised of creamy, tiny cheeses, such as Jasper Hill creamy Winnimere, that is emerging now, but the Alpines discussed here are the larger ones.

A shared characteristic is that Alpine-style cheesemakers cut the curds small, cook them slowly at low temperatures, and press the cheese to get rid of as much moisture as possible. They started doing this because the wheels needed to last all winter long. Alpine families depended on the wheels for nutrition during the cold months when milk quantities were limited, and drier cheeses would last longer. Many continue to do this because during the slow curd-cooking process, warm notes such as walnut, onion, or caramel translate to the cheese.

Another Alpine practice that has shaped the taste of the cheeses here is seasonal grazing. For centuries Alpine wheels were made only with milk from animals grazing on high summer pastures. This made it so the grasses in the lowlands could be harvested and stored for winter when it was too cold for the cattle to be taken to pasture. Flavor-wise, it made it so spring and summer cheeses tasted more herbal, floral, and even fruity due to what the animals were eating while grazing. More and more cheesemakers Stateside are taking up this practice today.

Influenced by European immigrants from Alpine regions who moved to the United States, these practices have inspired cheesemakers in all realms. Like cheddar, Alpine cheeses have had a huge place in the United States. Some of the most inspired Alpine cheeses have been Beaufort, Gruyère, Comté, Savoie Tommes, Emmenthaler, and Fontina. Their wheels may have shrunk a little once they got here, but they'll always be big in our eyes.

Cobb Hill Ascutney Mountain, Vermont

"We've entered into the twentieth century with these presses," says smiling cheesemaker Jeanne Kilbride, pointing at Cobb Hill's recent

COBB HILL ASCUTNEY MOUNTAIN

purchase in the corner. Made of thick pieces of lightly stained wood, the antiquated yet highly functional press inspired by Dutch versions made in the mid-1800s enables the company to form not just fifteen or sixteen, but seventeen or more wheels. At one time.

Cobb Hill is a simultaneously traditional yet modern 270-acre cohousing establishment and enterprise in Hartland, Vermont. Just some of the things that make up Cobb Hill are: sixty-four people; twenty-four homes; solar-powered water and electricity; high-speed DSL internet; fjord horses to plow the fields; compost toilets that "flush" with a handful of wood shavings; and individually owned enterprises including but not limited to an Icelandic sheep meat business and Cobb Hill Cheese.

Decidedly an ode to rural Vermont like the cohousing development itself, Cobb Hill's Ascutney Mountain is named after the state's second-highest peak (and popular jump-off point for hang gliders). With a slightly orange rind that comes from being rubbed down with a saltwater brine, Ascutney is a buttery, nutty, rich, firm wheel with occasional onion and fruity green apple tones.

Although Ascutney was originally inspired by the Swiss greats such as Appenzeller and Emmenthaler, Cobb Hill is all for improv. The original owner was big on experimentation, and Kilbride, one of the three current cheesemakers who joined the team after hearing at an Obama rally in 2008 that "cheese at Cobb needed help," says Ascutney isn't chained to scientific method or firm recipes. It is based almost entirely on time, not pH measurements. Wheels are made throughout the year, and based on what the Jersey cows are eating or how the cheesemakers are feeling that day; hence, the taste differs greatly from sharp and fruity to creamier and subtle.

The general method for Ascutney goes likes this: First, the milk is heated to ninety-three degrees, cultures are added, and the milk is left alone so bacteria can develop for around half an hour. Then vegetable rennet is added to make the curd. When the curd has firmed, the cheesemakers cut it into tiny pieces as is typical with Alpine wheels—"rice size," says Kilbride, or about a quarter of an inch—much smaller than for cheddar or even Pecorino-style cheeses. Then they cook the curds on low heat for about an hour. This helps obtain a smooth and dry paste in the final wheel.

Next, the curds are scooped and hooped into plastic molds. Many Alpine or Alpine-inspired cheeses such as Beaufort or Pleasant Ridge Reserve (and many Goudas) are pressed under their own whey right before molding to help develop acidity levels. Acidity levels in some mountain Alpine cheeses can be low, as the raw milk rarely sits long enough to develop certain microbes that later aid in lactic acid development. But this Emmenthaler-inspired cheese skips this step.

After going into molds, Ascutney is pressed, the Dutch way, for a day or two, then moved to racks in an aging room to mature. Some four-month-old wheels are then transferred to Jasper Hill Cellars to age because Cobb Hill lacks enough room to store all they make (making a larger cheese cave would require that the cohousing development decide whether the community wants a dairy addition). Others are kept until they hit the optimum seven-to-eight-month mark.

Especially as it matures, Ascutney can take a pretty big wine. Bordeaux, Zinfandels, and Rhone Valley Grenache, Syrah, and Mouvedre blends (otherwise known as GSMs) are all fair game. A well-rounded cheese, Ascutney also likes its beers big, too. Brown ales and rich Belgians are its favorites.

Several other Emmenthaler- or Gruyère-inspired cheeses to try if Ascutney isn't available near you (look for it, though, since it likes to make appearances) are Veldhuizen Family Farm's Greens Greek Gruyère from Dublin, Texas; Marcoot Jersey Cave Aged Forest Alpine from Greenville, Illinois; and Consider Bardwell's Rupert from West Pawlet, Vermont (all are regionally available and many can be mail-ordered).

Uplands Cheese Company Pleasant Ridge Reserve, Wisconsin

Make it past customs with Uplands Pleasant Ridge in your suitcase when visiting cheesemongers abroad and you'll have a friend more loyal than a golden retriever. Name it as your favorite domestic cheese in France and you'll be taught the handshake that will allow you into the most exclusive underground *fromage* salons in Paris. Ask domestic cheesemakers for their inspirations, and 99.65 out of 100 times, you'll see eyes glistening and lips mouthing the word "Uplands."

Made from the raw milk from a mixed herd of cows eating only spring and summer grasses in Dodgeville, Wisconsin, Pleasant Ridge demonstrates a commitment to excellence in the American cheese movement. Uplands proved to the world that with a hell of a lot of passion and obsessive attention to detail, seasonality, and cow breeding, American cheesemakers can produce cheese that can knock even a true Alpine wheel out of the water.

Modeled after Beaufort, a cheese made in the French Alps, Pleasant Ridge is an eight-pound wheel with a beeswax-colored center and a rusty orange rind. It has a semifirm paste similar to Comté or Beaufort and is as smooth as a piece of lacquered wood. It tastes like pineapple, yeasty and buttery brioche, and the lemony grass of Wisconsin pastures when the fields are emerald.

Uplands takes great pains to ensure that flavor. Although not the first modern American cheesemaker to restrict making their cheese to spring and summer, when the grass imparts its brightest flavors and gives a rich, buttery color to the milk, Uplands co-owners and original cheesemakers Michael and Carol Gingrich (co-owners Dan and Jeanne Patenaude focused on the grazing practices and cattle) set a benchmark in 2003 by deciding that summer was the only time they would make this cheese every year because they wanted the best flavors or nothing at all.

Yet Uplands doesn't stop at seasonal grass. Current cheesemaker Andy Hatch thinks about how they can get the most out of milk far before the cow reaches the field. Specifically, he thinks about what he can do with breeding.

Unlike many American and nearly all European Alpine cheese-makers who stick to one type of animal breed (appellation laws dictate the breed in the case of Europe), Hatch believes that the more milk diversity, the more complex the milk. All cow's milk is different—some, such as Jerseys and Ayshires, have more butterfat in their milk. Others, such as Dutch belted, have more protein or smaller fat globulins. To get a good sampling of all the different breeds' milk goodness, Uplands mixes it up in the field. They inseminate cows with imported semen like that of Alpine Tarenteise until they get the perfect mix that lends Pleasant Ridge such complexity.

Back in the creamery, Hatch preserves that complexity. Hatch never pasteurizes his milk because he believes it would kill the flavor he's worked to obtain in the field and through breeding. Instead, he heats the milk slowly on very low heat, encouraging ambient bacteria and local microflora, highlighting even more of the milk's flavors and regional qualities.

The final step that sets Uplands apart from so many other cheese-makers is its affinage. The act of affinage is when a trained cheese specialist finishes or manages the final maturation and flavoring of cheese by flipping it, washing it, and babying it. That person may or may not be the cheesemaker. Proper affinage requires special attention to the needs of the cheese, and a good affineur can coax flavors out of a cheese that were previously reticent. Trained in cheesemaking and affinage in Austria, Norway, Italy, and France, Hatch considers the final step in cheesemaking more than just sending wheels with a little extra love.

He has three separate aging rooms for different stages of affinage and even babies the brine with which he washes down Pleasant Ridge Reserve. One brine for each stage—the initial wash down, the next couple months of maturation, and the final push in the room filled with bright orange Uplands beauties. In each room, Hatch tends the cheese as if it were his firstborn. He knows its optimal scents and textures at each stage of development and watches his cheeses like a daddy hawk. When I was in the aging room taking pictures and reached out to touch a Pleasant Ridge wheel, Hatch laughed and said that I shouldn't touch the aging wheels because he wasn't sure "where that camera has been." "Really?" I asked, decked out in a hair net, lab coat, and Wellingtons. "Well"—he shrugged—"I don't want something bad to happen to the cheese."

Pairing with a cheese that has such a curated mix of pronounced and subtle flavors can be tricky. Choose a wine that's too light, and you'll bore Pleasant Ridge. Choose something too big or spicy such as a Central Coast Rhone blend and you'll loose the nuances of the wheel. The best bet is to go with a fruity wine. I like it with a Riesling—dry or sweet or a round, citrusy Roero Arneis. For reds, go fruity and noncompetitive. A lightly aged Zinfandel with slightly less pronounced fruit notes fares surprisingly well, as does a lighthearted California Pinot Noir.

Other Alpine, perhaps even Beaufort-inspired, American cheeses to try are Spring Brook's Tarentaise from Reading, Vermont; Thistle Hill Tarentaise from Pomfret, Vermont (one or the other is available in most states); Doe Run Dairy Seven Sisters from Chester County, Pennsylvania (mainly found on the East Coast); and Pedrozo Dairy Blondie's Best from Orland, California (small amounts available nationwide).

Sequatchie Cove Farm Cumberland, Tennessee

That the main reason why Sequatchie Cove Farm cheesemaker Nathan Arnold decided on a Savoie-style tomme was its approachability is no surprise. A soft-spoken yet talkative man with kind eyes, Arnold is immediately likable himself. That he was passionate enough about cheese to make such a tomme with characteristics that can be articulated beyond "semisoft" or "great in mac and cheese" is also telling of his character. He could talk for hours about how he makes Cumberland and what the style means to him, yet would never once mention it's one of the greatest Alpine-style tommes outside Savoie.

Located in Sequatchie, Tennessee, Sequatchie Cove Farm is a diversified 300-acre farm that sells pasture-grazed meats, eggs, garden plants, vegetables and fruits, and of course, cheese. It's here that Arnold makes Cumberland, an example of Savoie-Alps cheesemaking and an expression of Southern *terroir*.

Cumberland is a three-inch-high, seven-pound, semisoft wheel. Its rind is a plush variegated quilt of molds in browns, grays, white, and the occasional orange, and its paste is the color of a peeled banana.

The taste varies from season to season like all grass-fed milk cheeses, but because Cumberland's identity is so defined by ambient molds (the ones that color the rind), its flavors differ greatly from wheel to wheel. Sometimes the molds are subdued and the cheese tastes livelier, more citrus-like, and grassier. Other times the buttery paste tastes earthier, a little like peanut butter, and finishes with a bite. In my eyes, these differences make the cheese even more exciting than waiting to see what new spin Martha Stewart will put on Christmas decorations this year.

Except that it's made with whole milk instead of skimmed, Cumberland's production is all Savoie style. Savoie tommes are subtle, semisoft (mainly cow's milk), pressed cheeses with thick, soft rinds that were originally made with milk after cream was removed to make rich dairy products such as butter. Like most Savoie tommes (*tomme* means "wheel"), Cumberland starts with raw milk, to which Arnold adds cultures and lets sit for a little over twenty-four hours.

The Tennessee Department of Agriculture wouldn't let Arnold use the copper kettles traditional in the Alps. "I told them they had been using them for years in France, even in other states in the U.S., without any problems, but," he sighs, "they weren't convinced." So he makes do with a stainless steel version of the same kettle. Next he adds a single strain of rennet, lets it coagulate, and cuts the curd by hand with a curd harp.

Then he stirs the curds, heating them on low for around an hour to both release moisture so the wheels can age longer and compensate for the additional butterfat in the whole milk. At this point he does something typical of an Alpine-style cheese—he pours off some of the whey, puts a weighted plate in the vat over the warm curds, and presses them under the remaining, and also still warm, whey. This gives the cheesemaker control over acidity and also helps to bind the curds. Pressing the curds under the warm whey knits them together better than just pressing them at room temperature after they've been put in molds. Many other cheesemakers concerned with getting a smooth paste also use this method. Then Arnold tilts the kettle to pours off the rest of the whey (which is pumped directly outside to feed the farm's happy pigs), takes the curds that have formed into blocks under pressure, and fits them into molds. They get brined eight hours later.

Then, it's off to the caves. After the wheels have been brined, they're transferred to Sequatchie Cove's cave—an old water tower that has been converted into an aging room that controls humidity and temperature through a geothermic system involving cell blocks, water filters and reservoirs, and air socks. The molds develop here.

Arnold brushes the wheels down with salt water every day for the first couple weeks to encourage yeast growth and keep pH levels optimum for rind growth. After the gray, brown, and ivory colors start showing up, he slows the brushing to under once a week. Arnold says he doesn't want his cave quite as furry-moldy as those in Savoie, but he doesn't want to discourage ambient molds either.

Letting the molds develop is part of the charm that led Arnold to the Savoie style in the first place. All villages in the region have their own tommes, and Arnold wanted to put his own Tennessee touch on this versatile cheese.

Cumberland is great on a cheese board with crunchy whole wheat bread and an onion marmalade (see page 114), but it's also great cooked, too. "It's complex," says Arnold, "but not so hard to get that a three-year-old wouldn't eat it." Melted, it adds an earthy touch to a fondue.

Have with a light, creamy white with good acidity such as one from the Savoie—a Jacquère or Roussane—or with Rhone Valley white or unoaked or lightly oaked Chardonnay. Light reds could also pass here, but whites are better. A Belgian tripel is also a good bet.

Other good Savoie-style tommes to try are Cherry Grove Farm's Herdsman (less plush-moldy than Cumberland, available online and on the East Coast), from Lawrenceville, New Jersey; Meadow Creek Dairy's Appalachian (square-shaped, found in limited quanities nationwide) from Galax, Virginia; and Capriole's Old Kentucky Tomme (a much softer goat's milk style) from Greenville, Indiana.

Caramelized Onion and Mustard Seed Marmalade

MAKES 1–1½ CUPS

The sweetness of caramelized onions cooked in bacon fat and the pop provided from the mustard seeds and lemon juice make for a marmalade that can stand up to the buttery pineapple flavors in Pleasant Ridge Reserve (even extra aged). It also pairs well with other semifirm or Alpine-style cheeses. Serve with Pleasant Ridge Reserve and bread or crackers to taste, and keep any extra for sandwiches the next day.

2 teaspoons mustard seed, to be soaked overnight
2 teaspoons apple cider vinegar
1½ medium-sized yellow onions
2 slices bacon, medium diced
¼ teaspoon salt
1 tablespoon butter (optional)
2 tablespoons lemon juice
additional salt and pepper to taste

Mix the mustard seed and vinegar in a bowl, cover with plastic wrap, and let soak for 8 hours or overnight.

Cut off the tops and bottoms of the onions. Remove the outer skin layer. Set the onion on a cutting board with a cut side as the base. Slice the onion in half. Take one half of the onion, flip so the interior portion is on the cutting board, and slice in half, keeping both halves together. Now rotate the onion so the slice is vertical and cut the onion half into thin slices horizontally. Continue with all halves.

Place the bacon in a cast-iron skillet or heavy-bottomed medium-sized sauté pan. Turn the heat to low and cook until the fat starts to render from the bacon, stirring occasionally to scrape any brown bits from the bottom of the pan. Add the onion and salt, turn up the heat to medium high, and cook for 3–5 minutes until the onion has golden edges, stirring occasionally. Turn the heat to low and cook for an additional 20–25 minutes, stirring occasionally, until the onions have gained a silky, uniformly golden color and are very sweet. Add butter as needed if the onion starts to stick to the pan. Add the mustard seed and lemon juice and cook for 5 more minutes. Remove from heat. Cool and serve.

The U.K. Influence

• • • • •

Miners, Bandages, and Lard

While English delicacies such as beans on toast have never rung the culinary bell in the United States, British cheese has had a huge influence on the American culinary scene. Especially cheddar.

As thoroughly explored in *American Farmstead Cheese* by Paul Kindstedt, most Puritans who crossed the pond from Britain to make New England their home were from East Anglia—a cheesemaking region that focused on making big, durable, low-moisture cheeses. As more Europeans with dairy penchants immigrated to North America and colonizers in the West Indies clamored for a taste of home via cheese exports, demand for cheese was high, and New Englanders used their knowledge to fulfill the need. At this point, cheese was still at a farmstead level. Then in 1851, an industrialist named Jesse Williams created machinery that mechanized cheesemaking.

Within a matter of years, cheese changed forever. Women no longer made commercial cheese in home kitchens, men were making it in factories, and most of it was cheddar. Because cheddar, a cheese created in Somerset, England, in the town of Cheddar, was so popular in England at the time and cheese economics were poor in the United States due to the Civil War, East Coast producers set up factories to produce mass amounts of the cheese style to ship to the United Kingdom. Cheddar has reigned the king of American cheese ever since.

It's speculated it was around this time that some cheddars became orange. Some factories added annatto seed to the milk to dye the wheels the color of a popular cheddar in England at the time. Others were emulating the color of a pastured cow's milk—bright yellow leaning toward orange. Others say that Midwestern areas such as Wisconsin added annatto to differentiate their cheddar from East Coast versions.

An easily transportable cheese, cheddar was perfect for a society so invested in work. Wrapped up for lunch, a piece of cheddar is nutritious, fills workers' stomachs, and keeps well at room temperature until the lunch bell rings.

Cheddar, and to a much lesser extent a few noncheddars such as Caerphilly from the Somerset region, have helped to build the foundation of American cheese. Along the way many different styles, colors, and flavors have been introduced. The meaning of the word "cheddar" will be discussed in the next focus. Despite the bastardization or two of the original recipe, cheddar and its friends have made a lasting impression on American culture. Cases in point: North American cheesemakers are now making artisan versions that rival the Brits', and "cheddar" has entered the hip hop lexicon as just another way to say "money."

Fiscalini Clothbound Cheddar, California

Made in the quiet agricultural San Joaquin Valley, where 50 percent of California's produce is grown and two-thirds of the radio stations are Christian themed or Spanish speaking, Fiscalini Cheddar is one of the most modest cheeses in the country. Although it pairs stunningly with whiskey, you'll never find Fiscalini around town with a drink in its hand boasting that it's won more cheese awards than Quincy Jones has Grammys.

Of course, it doesn't need to. With a texture that crumbles lightly when sliced and a golden hue untouched by artificial coloring, Fiscalini shows what real farmstead cheddars are made of. Meaty, buttery, salty, and with a seductive earthy flavor that would make a French winemaker blush, this fifty-pound-plus wheel is known as one of the best cheddars in the world.

But what makes something a cheddar? After the proper cultures, rennet, and acids are added to the milk and the curds coagulate, the first step toward a fine wheel of cheddar is called "cheddaring."

Instead of taking the curds after they separate from the whey, pressing them under whey, or putting them in molds or cheesecloth, the cheddarmaker adds another crucial step. Cheesemakers such as Fiscalini's Mariano Gonzalez, who trained at Shelburne Farms in Vermont, screech the process to a halt after the curds are drained, pile them on one another, and let them hang out. As the curds sit there shooting the breeze, their lactose (milk sugar) converts into lactic acid. After a couple hours, the lactic acid intensifies. That trademark "sharp" tang that tickles your tongue with cheddar? That's the provoked lactose to lactic acid conversion, which takes place during the cheddaring.

Gonzalez and his assistants taste and measure acidity levels every few minutes. After he senses the curd is sufficiently tangified, they salt and stir the curds to stop the cheddaring process. Then they show off their guns.

Gonzalez and his team pack and press hundreds of pounds of cheese into machine presses. And this ain't no little pressing. They use press machines and their own body weight to squeeze the remaining whey out of the wheels to encourage a tight, smooth paste. To get an idea of how much effort this takes, if you bring your grandmother who lives in Modesto with you to the farm, she'll at this point tell the cheesemakers how strong they are and will repeat this every five minutes until they're finished.

Once the wheels are pressed, it's bandage and lard time. First, the cheddars are wrapped with muslin cloth, otherwise called a bandage. Then, they're larded up. According to Paul Kindstedt, PhD, author of *Cheese and Culture*, a book that focuses on the history of cheese in Western civilization, the practice of wrapping and larding (or buttering) cheddars probably originated independently in the United States. Enrobing the cheese first in cloth, then sealing the deal by covering the wheel in a tasty fat, helped to prevent moisture loss and protect the cheese from pests and harsh elements that were especially prevalent in New England. A combo of cloth wrapping and lard produces the layered, earthy flavors in Fiscalini, and now in some British Cheddars, whose cheesemakers picked up the practice.

Sixteen months or so later, after the cheesemakers have flipped the slippery wheels enough to evenly distribute moisture (and so that they probably never want to look at a pig again), Fiscalini Cheddar is ready.

Pair with brown liquor (bourbon, whiskey, tequila), darker brews, a heavily oaked Chardonnay or Viognier, Zinfandel, Grenache-Syrah-Mourvedre blends, or Bordeaux. According to Venezuela-born Gonzalez, Fiscalini also pairs especially well with a soccer game.

Bandage-wrapped cheddar has layers of flavors that will never be found in a commodity block, so if you have written off this cheese family because of what's in your grocery aisle, give it another chance. If you don't spot Fiscalini near you, try Cabot Clothbound aged by Jasper Hill from Greensboro, Vermont; Shelburne Farms Clothbound Cheddar from Shelburne, Vermont; Bleu Mont from Blue Mounds, Wisconsin; or Avalanche's Goat Cheddar from Paonia, Colorado. The first two are readily available across the country, Bleu Mont and Avalanche being much more sparsely distributed.

Landaff Creamery Landaff, New Hampshire

"I was hoping they'd come up and use the brush so you could see how much they love it," Doug Erb said, referring to the three-foot plastic back scratcher hanging from the barn ceiling for his Holsteins.

Landaff

"But they, ah . . . they've got other instincts right now," he added, laughing.

A couple of heifers were getting in a little mounting practice before breeding, which Erb assured us was just a few days out. He shrugged his shoulders. Such is the life on a cow farm.

Dairy farmers first and cheesemakers second, Doug and Debbie Erb run a dairy and cheesemaking operation in the White Mountains of Landaff, New Hampshire. They started making Landaff in 2008 in a last-attempt effort to add value to their milk in a high-stakes market where it can be impossible to break even. Selling Landaff not only helped them to keep their land, cows, and business, but gave the Erbs another passion, and gave us a beautiful Caerphilly-style cheese.

Landaff is made from the raw milk of Erb's closed breed of Holsteins, whose lineage can be traced back to the original Holstein herds brought from Holland to the United States in the mid-ninteenth century. The cheese has a thick, stony brown and gray rind that occasionally seductively edges into the paste. Depending on the season and whether the cows have fresh grass to munch on, the paste ranges from bright manila yellow to a creamy off-white. Brighter, livelier, and grassier than a lawn just dusted with MiracleGro, Landaff has a lively tart yet sweet buttermilk taste typical of a Welsh Caerphilly-style cheese that grows earthier as it ages.

At first uncertain what style cheese to make, the Erbs went Welsh after Deb discovered that Caerphilly was made in a town also called Landaff in the United Kingdom. Shortly thereafter, Doug packed his bags to train with third-generation Caerphilly producer Chris Duckett in Somerset, England. Caerphilly is like a cross between a lively, less tangy, young cheddar and a plush-rinded, milky, and approachable Savoie tomme, but with a crumblier texture. The result of his Welsh tenure, studying at the Vermont Institute for Artisan Cheese in Burlington, and learning from the Cellars at Jasper Hill crew in

Greensboro, who age and market Landaff, is a Caerphilly that combines traditional methods with Duckett's production insights.

Two things that make Caerphilly and Landaff distinct from other cheeses, says Doug, are texturing and pressing.

"Texturing" is a labor-intensive Welsh method in which the cheesemaker recuts and salts the curds by hand with knives to form random-sized, moist pieces after the curds (already previously cut to expel whey) have reknit. This helps produce Caerphilly's moist, somewhat crumbly yet cohesive texture.

Proper pressing is also crucial. It was so important to Doug that when he visited Duckett's operation, he measured all the pullies and angles of the third-generation Somerset cheese press, returned, and hired a local engineer to create a low-tech, horizontal (yet slightly angled) machine that applies, as Doug says, "the exact same coefficient of adhesion" as the one in Somerset. Even though Doug aims for a firmer paste than the original so Landaff will also be a good melting cheese, his machine replicates the "soft press" that inspires Caerphilly's moist texture.

Reportedly originally a cheese made at home for miners to take to work, Caerphilly has a composition that speaks to its history. Its random-sized curds, soft press, and thick rind that miners could grasp without worrying about dirtying the paste reflect the times and means of production. England allocated most cheese milk to cheddar to aid the war effort during World War II, and farmhouse Caerphilly fell out of production as a result, so Caerphilly never grew as popular as cheddar in the United States. But it's a style that's now growing as cheesemakers are relearning its value.

A couple other fantastic Caerphilly-style cheeses to try beyond the readily available Landaff are Cobb Hill's Four Corners from Hartland, Vermont; Bleu Monts Caerphilly (made seasonally) from Blue Mounds, Wisconsin; and Winter's Caerphilly from Winters, California (all limited production, but ask your cheese shops if they can find them). More are being produced as of this writing. Try with an English ale; a high-acidity, interesting white such as Riesling or Robialla Gialla; or a red such as Pinot Noir or Gamay. Toss in some olives, ham, and bread for a complete miner-inspired meal.

Beehive Barely Buzzed, Utah

Cheese geeks often organize cheddars into two worlds. There's the glorious bandage-wrapped, larded-up, old-world-style wheels that represent all that's virtuous about artisanal cheese. Then there are the modern, machine-made, tasteless, tangerine orange rectangles that make large corporations (not dairy farmers) millions of dollars.

In reality, there are entire cheddar lands in between.

With its Barely Buzzed, Beehive Cheese shows how science and innovation can mix harmoniously with tradition. Utilizing a hybrid British farmhouse–modern method and flavor additions that are entirely new school, Barely Buzzed is an original American homage to artisan cheddar.

Covered in a finely ground, fluffy blend of ground South American, Central American, and Indonesian coffee beans and dried lavender buds, Barely Buzzed is a "flavored cheddar." What sets it apart from so many other mediocre "flavored" cheeses is that rather than mixing the additions into the milk to mask subpar dairy, Beehive enhances its already great milk by pressing the grounds and lavender on the rind after the cheese is made.

When you slice into Barely Buzzed's rind, coffee and lavender buds tumble off the rind and stick to the cheese's light yellow, smooth, semisoft paste. A first taste reveals primary coffee and lavender tones.

After the initial caffeinated punch (skip the rind—too strong), a chocolate, earthier, meatier flavor emerges. It's a rich cheese whose flavors permeate the entire mouth. In wine terms, Barely Buzzed has a long finish.

Like many great inventions, Barely Buzzed was a happy accident. One of the company's owners, Tim Welsh, had leftover coffee around from his brother's coffee company. He decided to add dried lavender that was hanging out on his spice rack to the grounds then pat the mix on two two-pound wheels of Beehive's original cheddar. Just because. Then he put that, and a maraschino chocolate version with which he was also fooling around, away and forgot about them.

Six months later, the team ran into the experiments in the back of the aging room and sliced them open. They loved the Barely Buzzed. The maraschino cheddar, not so much. On a whim, they entered the coffee beauty in the American Cheese Society Conference competition, and it garnered so many accolades that a market in Texas ordered 4,000 pounds. Welsh, who had only two ounces, ramped up production by a pound or two.

To make their flavored cheeses such as Barely Buzzed, Beehive uses the University of Utah's original "Promontory" recipe (based on a cheddar style), slaps on flavorings, then vacuum packs them in plastic. Even though cheddar lovers now through and through, what initially pushed Welsh and his brother-in-law partner toward this style was the University of Utah's offer of full research and recipe support if they went commercial with the Promontory recipe. The first-time cheesemakers jumped at the opportunity.

A few things make Beehive's modern Promontory recipe different from a farmhouse British style. One, instead of using only traditional cheddar cultures, Beehive starts with cultures that produce a fruitier flavor. Two, they use Jersey cow's milk rather than Holstein. Three, instead of letting the wheels develop natural rinds or using cloth or fat to protect the cheese from drying and pests, they age theirs in a plastic bag.

Beehive also doesn't call their cheeses "cheddars." They've entered and won awards in that category, though, and there's no mistaking the flavor profile: tangy, sharp, buttery, and sweet.

As with the farmhouse styles, eat Barely Buzzed with the clean flavors of a sparkling wine, a fruity Zinfandel or American Cabernet or Merlot, or a chocolate stout.

Other cheddar-inspired (but less flavored) cheeses or cheddars to try that aren't bandage-wrapped are Beecher's Flagship from Seattle, Washington (more earthy, nutty, widely available); Spring Hill Goat Cheddar from Petaluma, California (more citrus notes, available on-line and in California); 5 Spoke Creamery's Browning Gold (sweeter, with less cheddar tang, well distributed) from Westchester, New York; and Hook's 5 and 10 years cheddars (no rind, takes on amino acid crystals the older it gets, well distributed), from Mineral Point, Wisconsin.

Landaff and Celery Root
Beer Soup

As a California native, I've always been curious about the classic beer-cheese soup served in Midwestern areas. Some recipes use potatoes as a thickeners, others use cornstarch, and others use roux. Some chefs spice up the dish with pimentos, onion powder, or chiles. I shaped this recipe around Landaff—so I went with earthy potatoes, celery root, and leeks instead of onions to avoid overwhelming the cheese, and used bacon as the cooking fat. Another Caerphilly-style cheese, or a bandage-wrapped cheddar, would work, too. Use a light beer such as a saison; avoid IPAs or those with bitter finishes.

2 leeks with white stems 4–5 inches long
1 pound celery root
3 pieces bacon, small diced
2 celery ribs, medium diced
1 bottle light beer
1 pound potatoes, peeled, large dice
3½ cups chicken broth
1 teaspoon fresh thyme, chopped
1 bay leaf
¾ pound Landaff, shredded, without rind
salt and pepper to taste

Slice off the bottoms of the leeks so that the vegetable's rings are revealed. Then cut off the top dark green part, about 4 or 5 inches from the bottom. Dispose of both parts. Slice the remaining leek lengthwise, then into half-rings about a half-inch thick. Wash well under running water to rid the leek of any sand. Set aside to drain.

Wash the celery root then cut off the top and bottom and

trim off its rough outer peel to reveal the white inner root. Cut into large cubes. Set aside.

Put the bacon in a medium-sized soup pot with a heavy bottom. Turn on the heat to low to render the fat. Cook for 10 minutes. Add the leeks to the bacon and its fat. Turn the heat to medium-low and cook until the leeks start to turn translucent, or for about 10 minutes. Raise the heat to medium, add the celery, and cook for 5 minutes. Deglaze the mixture by pouring one-fifth of the beer into the pan and scrapping any stuck bits from the bottom of the pan.

Add the celery root and potatoes to the pot. Stir, then add the rest of the beer and the chicken stock. Add the thyme and bay leaf. Bring to a boil then reduce to a simmer. Cook for 30 minutes or until potatoes mash against the side of the pot with the back of the spoon.

Cool for 10 minutes, then blend until somewhat smooth in a blender. If you don't have a blender, mash the soup with a potato masher in the pot. Return to the pot, bring to low heat, and add the shredded cheese. Stir until melted. Salt and pepper to taste and serve.

Aged Sheep's Milk

· · · · ·

Manchego, Pecorino,
and the Pyrenees

Since the beginning of cheesemaking in the United States, this country has been all about the cows. Those cute, fuzzy little sheep dotting the Sonoma landscape for years before the state's first sheep's milk dairy was certified in 1990? They ended up on your Easter plate or with their wool woven into your sweater.

When early Europeans settled here, they brought cattle. Most moved to areas with wide-open spaces and the occasional rolling hill, which worked well for mellow cows, who preferred existing on level areas that required little effort. As large-format wheels that required copious amounts of milk such as cheddar gained prominence, it made commercial sense to continue focusing on cows—who, unlike sheep, provided abundant, familiar-tasting milk supplies.

It wasn't until Vermont Shepherd in Westminster West, Vermont, started making cheese with their sheep's milk around 1993 that Americans really considered sheep's milk for cheesemaking. And they only just considered it. After those cheesemaking pioneers proved that not only were sheep indeed milkable (gasp!), but their milk made amazing cheese, others slowly took notice. Well, ideas were planted at least.

Eventually more sheep's milk dairies started appearing here and there. Because sheep's milk was still so unusual and its cheeses still so foreign to most, people looked to imported standards to figure out what to make. Manchego, Pecorino, and Basque wheels were the go-tos. Semifirm styles were still dominant.

While the British themselves were the ones teaching the cheddar-making process in the States, learning how to make most sheep's milk cheese here required a visit to Italy, France, or Spain, or at least looking up a recipe in a book. Most Basque immigrants (who mainly settled on the West Coast in the nineteenth and early twentieth centuries) were involved in other ventures such as shepherding or gold mining, and those who came from La Mancha or Italy weren't spear-heading a sheep cheese movement. Granted, the U.S. government also enacted immigration exclusion acts during the early twentieth century with quotas on European immigrations and beyond that severely rescricted the number of immigrants from areas where shepherding was an honored profession. So off American cheesemakers went, in great concentrations, to the Spanish and French Basque Pyrenees mountains and to Italy.

Thankfully for lovers of nutty, buttery, rich sheep's milk cheeses, these wheels have found a happy home in the cheese case. And with the help of sheep conferences, cooperatives, and institutes such as those in Wisconsin and elsewhere, the wheels will keep growing—not in size (sheep give less milk and need to rest if they are to live up to our cheesy expectations), but in number.

Bellwether San Andreas, California

It wasn't until Bellwether cheesemaker Liam Callahan discovered in the early nineties that many of his and his family's favorite cheeses were made from sheep's milk, not cow's, that he figured he could put the milk from his family's ewes to good use. Milk type wasn't discussed much back then. If you were lucky enough to pick up an already-wrapped cheese that said "Manchego" or "Pecorino," you didn't ask questions. You took the cheese home and ate it.

Bellwether's San Andreas is a Pecorino-style cheese made in Sonoma, California. It's a three-pound wheel with curved sides and an orange rind that comes from a light washing. The paste is semifirm, with a crumbly, slightly lacy texture that slices, shaves, and melts well. Its sister, Pepato, is studded with black peppercorns.

Bellweather San Andreas

San Andreas tastes as lively as Sonoma looks during spring. It has a slightly tangy, buttermilk, lemony taste accompanied by flavors of fresh cream seasoned with freshly ground pepper and chives, topped off with a toasted walnut or two.

Bellwether was the first certified sheep's milk dairy in California in 1990. But even though they were certified and the company, started by Liam's mother in the late eighties, had been selling lamb, it didn't mean they knew what they were doing when they started making sheep's milk cheese. One of Callahan's favorite memories is of him chasing after ewes with a large insect net.

Callahan ended up making Pecorino instead of a Basque-style cheese or Manchego like others who were starting to make sheep's milk cheeses at the time because of his connections. Situated in the hills of Sonoma, the Callahan family had been selling their lamb to chefs around San Francisco. When trying to decide which type of cheese to craft, they hit the very strongly Italian-influenced culinary streets in the city at the time and asked chefs what they wanted to see in their kitchens. The answer was a local Pecorino.

So the Callahans left for Tuscany with a list of cheesemaker names and B-and-B addresses and came back with a wheel or two of cheese in their suitcases, liters of limoncello, magnums of Brunello (I'm making the booze part up, but let's keep this fantasy), and a passion for the cheese whose name translates to "of the sheep." They returned a couple times to perfect their recipe over the next four years. They visited cheesemakers, pinpointed how they wanted their cheese to differ from the archetype, and after refining their own practice, helped introduce sheep's cheese to Americans with San Andreas.

San Andreas is made very similar to a Pecorino. Callahan starts with raw milk brought to a higher temperature than many firm cheeses. Like Pecorino Toscano, San Andreas's curds aren't cooked or pressed later in the process to expel whey, so Callahan heats the milk high to rid curd moisture early on. He adds cultures and lets them ripen in the milk for half an hour, adds rennet, lets it set for thirty more minutes, then cuts the curd into what he calls "pecorino," or between pea- and rice-sized pieces. He then lets the curds rest quickly, stirs them, then fills the Pecorino forms. After a couple hours, they're sent to a cooler room, dry salted, then a day later sent to the long-term aging room. They're turned every day for the first week to promote even rind growth and prevent bottom heaviness, and washed with a saltwater brine solution.

Because the curds go straight into molds after they are cut, most of the cheese's acidity develops in the wheel. Much of the difference between San Andreas and Pecorino Toscano has to do with its low acidity (lack of sharpness). Low acid promotes a subtler mouthfeel, more moisture, and *Brevibacterium linens* development that is instigated by washing the rind (rarely, if ever, seen in a Pecorino).

The cheese's fresh flavors make it almost impossible to mess up when pairing. Any lighter beer works. Callahan likes San Andreas with Pinot Noirs and aged Cabernets. I agree and would go further in saying that it pairs well with any wine without residual sugar or that's not extremely plush such as a Zinfandel or California Syrah (although Pepato's peppery bite likes both).

San Andreas is also good heated. The high-moisture, semifirm cheese melts well and its lemony flavors help to lighten up a heavy-handed potato gratin or mac and cheese recipe. One of my favorite ways to serve it, though, is shaved over fava beans and drizzled with olive oil as is classic with Pecorino in Tuscany. Other Pecorino-styled cheeses that would fare equally well are Blackberry Farm Singing Brook from Walland, Tennessee (available through mail order); Black Sheep Creamery's fresh and aged Pecorinos from Chehalis, Washington (found mainly in the Pacific Northwest); and Bonnieview Farm's Coomersdale from Craftsbury, Vermont (available mainly on the East Coast and via mail order).

Barinaga Ranch Txiki, California

Marcia Barinaga's hair was still wet when she arrived half an hour late to the Sonoma Cheese Festival's "A Day in the Life of a Cheesemaker" panel. It was birthing season; no one was surprised. After handling a difficult delivery less than an hour earlier, when Barinaga pulled three babies from a pregnant ewe that nearly lost her life, the session moderator told us that Barinaga decided to hop in the shower. She was a perfect embodiment of the panel's title, session attendees all agreed.

Former journalist and geneticist Marcia Barinaga is the head cheesemaker and owner of Barinaga Ranch, an 800-acre spread that overlooks miles of Marin County countryside. It's one of the many farmstead sheep's milk dairies in the United States that pay homage to the Pyrenees, and Barinaga's cheeses reflect the strong influence of the Basque region on American cheese.

The Barinagas bought the ranch in 2001 because they wanted to raise sheep like Marcia's Basque family in Spain. To the glee of her Spanish cheesemaking shepherd relatives, eight years later, Barinaga made her first wheel of Txiki.

Modeled after the Basque shepherd cheese *Ossau Iraty* on the French side of the Pyrenees, and *Idiazabal* (the unsmoked version) on the Spanish side, Barinaga Ranch's Txiki is a raw milk cheese with a light orange-brown rind, a basket mold pattern, and buttery, nutty, grassy notes. It is Barinaga's version of a typical Pyrenees shepherd-style cheese. Bordering France and Spain, the Pyrenees mountain range is rough, steep terrain. Leading their ewes where cows would fear to tread to snack on the different seasonal plants, shepherds rule this turf. Here, they mainly focus on making small, semifirm, easily transportable sheep's milk cheeses with lightly washed rinds. Because they're just weighed down with other wheels to leech out moisture rather than with heavy presses, the pastes often have holes and retain a natural softness less akin to a Pecorino.

Like many other cheesemakers who look to the Pyrenees for inspiration, Barinaga honors Basque methods in her own way. American food safety regulations won't allow Barinaga to carry milking buckets straight from the hand-milked sheep into the cheese room like smaller cheesemakers in Basque Spain, but Barinaga uses the same cultures and cutting patterns, and stirs and cooks the curds the same way. She also aims for the same acidity levels, and even uses a gentle milk pump to imitate the region's hand milking methods to keep the milk fats intact. Even though she considered making Manchego or Pecorino styles, Barinaga felt the Basque family pull.

"My cousin who makes cheese in Spain and only speaks Basque recently emailed me, saying he was overjoyed with my decision to uphold the family tradition. I was so touched. It was like I came full circle."

This isn't hard to believe. Watching Barinaga with her ewes makes it hard to believe she ever did anything besides care for a flock. As she stops wide-eyed, mid-discussion, to check on a running sheep who "seems really alarmed," or climbs over a fence to examine a baby who "looks like her bad eye's bothering her," it's clear that Barinaga's first allegiance is to her sheep.

The only reminder of her former career in science is her discussion of the charts she creates for her new milkers so she can calculate their genetic value. Then, when a minute later her eyes tear up as she talks about the hardships of weaning the new babies from their mothers, one is reminded of the complexity of American cheese culture and its craftspeople. We are a place where a geneticist can be sensitive.

Txiki and its bigger sister, Brasseri, pair with smoked preserves, marinated peppers, low-oak Tempranillos, and a wide range of white wines such as Sauvignon Blanc or lightly oaked Chardonnays.

Also try Vermont Shepherd's Shepherd's Basket from Putney, Vermont (distributed nationally); Willow Hill Vermont Brebis from Milton, Vermont (available mainly on the East Coast); 3 Corner Battenkill Brebis from Shushan, New York (available in limited amounts nationwide and through mail order); and Garden Variety Moonflower from Royal Oaks, California (found mainly in California).

Shepherd's Way Farms Friesago, Minnesota

All it took was a randomly landed upon newspaper article to inspire the launching of Shepherd's Way Farms. For a while, editor and science writer Jodi Ohlsen-Read and her teacher husband, Steven Read, had been discussing ways they could simplify their life and focus on their family through a creative career, but didn't know how to do so until Steven stumbled on an article that raved about the glories of owning dairy sheep. Compelled by the idea of farming, keeping animals, and staying close to home for work, the duo bit the carrot and bought their first flock in 1994, no more than three months after Read picked up that fateful newspaper.

"That article stuck with him," says Ohlsen-Read. "It was kind of a crazy time to do it when we started, and people were confused when we said we were a sheep dairy back then, but now people don't even blink an eye."

The Reads make Friesago, a Manchego-style sheep's milk cheese, in Carver County, Minnesota. Named after the Friesan sheep breed that the family owns, Friesago has a black wax rind and an ivory white center. It looks like a Gouda but tastes like a Manchego. Its texture is smooth. Unlike a Manchego, it has a tight paste with no holes and is a semisoft consistency like Provolone so it melts well. Like a Manchego, it has a buttery flavor that comes from the sheep's butterfat-rich milk and a light meaty flavor. Subtle citrus and herbal notes help Friesago stand apart from its Spanish-inspired imports.

Friesago, like Shepherd's Way Farms, came to be through happenstance. The couple decided on a Manchego style because, as new cheesemakers competing with European imports that cost less than Shepherd's Way could even sell their milk, they needed to pick a cheese that was at once familiar but also unique in the American market. Next, they created the cheese's identifiable black wax rind because there was no support for anything else. No one around them knew anything about natural rinds in the early nineties, so if they messed up, they messed up alone.

Shepherd's Way starts out with anywhere from 2,500 to 4,000 pounds of milk to make thirty-five to fifty wheels of cheese. "Even making our small batches of Friesago," says Ohlsen-Read, "is a good-size workout." They pasteurize the milk at high temperatures very quickly, then cool the milk down (some say this flash process preserves flavors ordinarily lost in the milk through normal pasteurization), add cultures and rennet, and then cut the curd by hand. Then the curds are cooked on low, stirred, and pressed under the whey as is common with many Goudas and Alpine cheeses. Next they're molded by hand, pressed by stacking them five to six wheels high, brined for two to three days, waxed, then aged for three to four months.

It's mainly the cheesemaking part of owning a creamery that

Ohlsen-Read finds so rewarding. "It's magical," she says. "It's visceral, tangible, and incredibly rewarding to go from fluid milk to tangible cheese, and then to send it away and see it somewhere else."

After you take Friesago home from that somewhere else, you're going to need to consume it. Eat it fresh, on sandwiches, or melt it. It has a high enough moisture content so that it softens easily when heated and can add a buttery, meaty dimension to a cooked dish such as a quiche or gratin. If snacking on it with wine, have with nearly any white from a lean, mineral Sauvignon Blanc from the Sancerre region to a California Chardonnay, or enjoy with a variety of red domestic wines that have a softer finish, or with a Tempranillo from Spain. This is a friendly cheese that also likes beers from light to dark.

Friesago is readily available throughout the Midwest, many other parts of the country, and through mail order, but here are some likeminded cheeses to try: Garden Variety Black-Eyed Susan from Royal Oaks, California; Bleating Heart Sheep-O-Rama from Sebastopol, California (both mainly available in California only); and Cato Corner Womanchego from Colchester, Connecticut (pretty easy to find nationally).

Chicken Under a Brick with San Andreas Butternut Squash Purée

SERVES 4

My favorite way to cook chicken breasts at home is "under a brick" style. Applying pressure and flattening the breasts cooks the chicken in a fraction of the time, browns the meat, and keeps the skin extra crispy. If you don't happen to have bricks lying around, no problem. Place a large cast-iron or sauté pan over the breast and weigh it down with three or four cans from your pantry—it will be just as good. Keeping the chicken flavors simple highlights the warm fall and winter flavors in the butternut squash and San Andreas purée. Serve this with a side salad or your favorite vegetable, and a glass of Viognier or dry Riesling, and you have a full meal.

2 pounds acorn squash
2 tablespoons butter
1 tablespoon olive oil
4 chicken breasts, skin on, ribs removed
salt and pepper to taste
1 clove garlic, minced
8 ounces San Andreas, grated

Slice the stem and the bottom off the squash and discard. Peel the squash, then cut it in half and remove the seeds. Cut into 1-inch cubes. Place in a medium-sized saucepan and fill with water so the squash is covered by an inch. Bring to a boil, then reduce to a simmer and cook for 10–15 minutes, or until a fork easily pierces the squash. Drain. Puree the squash in a food processor or mash with a potato masher (more rustic, but just as tasty).

Warm a large sauté pan over medium heat. Once hot, add a tablespoon of butter and the olive oil. Liberally salt and pepper the chicken. Place the chicken in the skillet, skin side down, and weigh down with the bricks or another skillet. Cook for 6–7 minutes, flip the chicken over, and repeat. The chicken is done when it's poked with a skewer and the juices are no longer pink. Once finished, let sit for 4 minutes before serving.

While the chicken is cooking, melt 1 tablespoon of the butter on low heat in the saucepan. Add the garlic and cook for 2 minutes. Add the squash puree and stir, then add the cheese, stirring until melted. Cover and keep on low heat until the chicken is ready. When ready, spoon the puree over a plate, top with the chicken, and serve with your favorite vegetable.

Aged Goat's Milk Tommes

· · · · ·

Wheels and Squares

Tomme technically just means "round" or "cheese wheel." It's a French way to define a wheel that could roll from one end of a dinner table to the other. However, like the concept of "dancing" as expressed by various ages and backgrounds on wedding reception floors, tomme means different things to different folks.

Many people's understanding of tomme is based on the mountain-style cheeses of the Alps or the Pyrenees such as Tomme de Savoie or Petite Agour. These are cooked, pressed, semifirm wheels often with buttery-colored pastes. To some, any firm cheese made in cylindrical form over three or four inches high is a tomme. I've heard less general people call any old aged goat's or sheep's milk cheeses a tomme, no matter the size or shape. I'd even like to name my first child Tomme.

Because tomme can mean so many things, it can indicate very little. Using it as a descriptor can be as revealing as a wine salesperson describing a wine as "fruity."

For this chapter, I broadened the use of tomme to fit my needs. A lot. I'm using it here to refer to aged goat's milk cheese, period, as in "goat's milk cheese tommes." But I'm only borrowing the term, not redefining it. You may continue using it for whatever you want.

Here, a goat's milk cheese doesn't have to be tall. It doesn't have to be cylindrical or even wheel-like. It doesn't have to have any specific regional influence; it only has to be aged over two months and made of goat's milk. These tommes, or wheels, are about taking goat's milk beyond chèvre, aging it, and coaxing even more complexity from the milk. They're usually semisoft to hard. I have no doubt that the "wheels" of this genre are nearly great enough in number and style to make up their own categories respectively.

Twig Farm Square Cheese, Vermont

Within the first two minutes of meeting Twig Farm's cheesemaker Michael Lee, you might describe him as . . . occupied. "Why are you here?" he asks with furrowed eyebrows when his assistant reminds him that the two lovely women waiting near the make room have traveled across the country to visit cheesemakers such as himself.

It isn't until after you've walked with him for an hour to feed three separate goat herds in sweaty August weather and watched him down a glass of water in three seconds that you notice his lithe physique truly reflects the life of a man who runs a thirty-goat farm and creamery enterprise with only the help of an assistant cheesemaker and his business partner and wife, Emily Sunderman. The dude is tired. Busy. Clearly dehydrated. And then you hope to God you haven't wasted his time.

Twig Farm is located in West Cornwall, Vermont, in an area Lee says reminds him of Appalachian territory—covered with acorns, hickory, and limestone. It's here on this thirteen-acre goat farm that

Twig Farm Square Cheese

Lee; his assistant cheesemaker, Megan Sanchez; and his wife, Emily Sunderman, craft quite possibly the squarest goat cheese in the United States.

Twig Farm's Square Cheese looks like a slightly fuzzy rock anomaly that has been gently shaped into a square after sitting in a riverbed for centuries. Its rind is mottled gray and white with a light dusting of brown, and its center is semisoft and ivory. It tastes like goat's buttermilk topped off with cream—rich, creamy, lemony, lively, reminiscent of hazelnut, and slightly herbal depending on the season.

Square became square because Lee was "fed up with the circle shape." When Lee started making the cheese on his own, he made wheels to fit into cylinder molds but quickly tired of the forms. They were a pain. So he tossed them out and started wrapping them in cheesecloth and squishing them into boxy shapes.

A semisoft cheese with a lot of moisture, Square starts with raw milk from Twig's mainly Nubian herd. They cook the milk at low temperatures, add cultures and rennet, then ladle the curds into cheesecloth. Then they squish them by hand to form the square until just the right amount of whey is released so that the wheel can age successfully while still keeping a moist texture. This and the pressure from the tightly tied cheesecloth itself is the only pressure that Square gets—no stacking of wheels on top of another, no pressing machines.

Once they're formed, they go into a saltwater brine for around twelve hours for seasoning and for slowing down the lactose to lactic acid conversion process. Then they're sent to the cellar underneath Lee and Sunderman's house for three months. While becoming a mature Square underground, its rind changes. It goes from being covered occasionally with what Sanchez calls "silky cat fur" mucor mold (not good for soft-ripened cheeses, but "tomme" friendly) to being mottled with whatever good molds the season and conditions provide.

Lee ascribes the tastes, flavors, and molds of his wheels to the region. *Terroir* isn't just for Europe. The characteristics of cheeses are shaped by their immediate surroundings. Cheese is a product created entirely by mold and microflora. "The only reason this is what it is, is because of where it's made," he says.

The cheesemakers and goats also have something to do with it. It's clear after following Lee around for a day that he's not the type to waste his animals' milk. He values his goats and all the work that goes into them too much. When he sees his does, his eyes light up the way they do when he's asked about his son's drawing that's hanging on the cheese room wall—a picture of a sabertooth tiger pulling a cage.

"This is Little Brown," he says, introducing me to a kid, "and that is Brown over there, her mother . . . and that's Evelyn, and Crabcake, and that is Rosalyn. Rosalyn," he says gently, raising his voice an octave at a doe that isn't staying on the path back home with the rest of the herd, "I've had just about enough of that."

Although a highly practical artisan cheese, Square is a little fussy with alcohol. It likes its wines clean, preferring Sauvignon Blancs, Grüner Vetliners, and Verdejos to Chardonnays or Viogniers. It also likes its reds lean. Northern Italian reds such as Nebbiolos or juicy, low-oak reds from Germany or Austria such as Blauburgunder or Lemburger keep Square's acidity in line. Light beers and gins work best here, too.

If Twig Farm's Sqaure Cheese isn't available near you, some other great semifirm (nonsquare) goat wheels to try are Aridith Mae's Henry from Hallstead, Pennsylvania (very hard to find); Lazy Lady's Tomme Delay from Westfield, Vermont (available on the East Coast and sporadically beyond that); and Cabra Linda (has an unusual rind that gets white and bloomy with age) from Avalanche Cheese in Paonia, Colorado.

Bohemian Creamery Caproncino, California

If we went with a strict definition of a tomme being a taller, cylindrical cheese, how Bohemian Creamery's cheesemaker Lisa Gottreich says she's always pictured a tomme, Caproncino wouldn't fit the mold. But since we, Gottreich, and her business partner, Miriam Block, aren't too concerned with fitting the mold (unless it's their breast-shaped molds for their cheese aptly named "Bodacious"), we're going to roll with it.

Speckled with beige, black, and brown, Caproncino's rind brings to mind a natural-toned malted chocolate Easter egg. It also looks like a tiny stone wheel made in caveman times. If Pebbles Flintstone had a Radio Flyer, the wheels that would get her from one corner of her yard to the other would look like Caproncino. And she'd be the envy of other cave children.

Caproncino is the size of a bread plate and an inch-and-a-half tall. It has a smooth surface and a variegated rind. Inside the paste is ivory, semifirm, and hole-free. The flavor is mineral, clean, mild, and lightly lemony. Because of its fresh flavors and gentle touch, it's a cheese that could bring those scared of that "goaty" taste over to the chèvre-inspired side. Unlike some aged goat's milk wheels that might turn a beginner off with their intensity (this one has been aged for three to four months), Caproncino stays mellow and inviting.

Gottreich's inspiration for Caproncino was Italy's Asiago. Gottreich was bitten by the Italian bug while she was an exchange student in the country and lived off and on in Italy for six years. During her various careers before she settled on cheesemaking in Sebastopol and even today, in California, she teaches Italian at her local community college, and names her wheels accordingly in homage to the Italian styles that have influenced her the most.

Mild at its young age, Asiago is a cheese crafted around the Veneto Alpine region of Italy. It's traditionally made with cow's milk, but Gottreich wanted to go goat. She had already been a home cheesemaker for fifteen years and made everything from feta to a goat-style Stilton (she used knitting needles to pierce the blue vines) with the milk from her own goats before becoming a professional. Gottreich wanted to explore the Asiago tradition using the milk she was most familiar with. Plus, an Asiago style was dependable—a good thing for a new company.

An Asiago-style cheese starts like any other aged wheel. In the case of Caproncino, the milk is pasteurized. Then, cultures and rennet are added. Once the curds are firm enough, Gottreich cuts them into pea-sized pieces and then cooks them at around 110 degrees until they coagulate and clump into a rubbery consistency. Cooking them until they're "rubbery" expels much of the whey, meaning that more moisture is cooked out (more moisture = more inconsistent and more possibility for bacteria = more chances that things can go wrong) and makes Caproncino "a very forgiving cheese."

Next, she quickly "hoops" (molds) the curds. She puts them in forms and flips them every couple of hours. Then, they're pressed under a combination of their own weight and one-pound salt bags to rid more moisture before they're brined, air dried for several days, then sent to the aging room for three to four months.

While they age, the natural, stony speckled rind develops. Gottreich flips the wheels so the rind will develop evenly but only wipes them down minimally so ambient molds like the wild blue, powdery mold that grows in Somona County grasses can have their regional say with Caproncino.

One of the local chef's favorite ways to serve Caproncino, says Gottreich, is shaved over vegetables or pasta. Like Bellwether's San Andreas or Anchandinha's Capricious, it would fare well shaved over fava beans or chard. It also melts well on buttered sourdough walnut bread with fig jam, which would make for a fantastic panini.

I like Caproncino with dried figs, green olives, and a simple white wine such as a Melon de Bourgogne from Muscadet, or a Southwestern Gros Manseng blend from France. Nearly any Italian white works here, too—Trebbiano, Cortese, etc. Just stay away from oak because it will overwhelm the cheese's subtle flavors. The same goes for red wines—go light and breezy, for example, a Gamay or Northern Italian or Austrian red such as Grignolino or Zweigelt.

If Bohemian's Caproncino isn't found around you, some other good goat tommes to try are Asgaard Farm Au Sable Valley Tomme from Au Sable Forks, New York; and Aridith Mae's Henry from Hallstead, Pennsylvania (mainly available on the East Coast).

Fraga Farms Rio Santiam, Oregon

It took three years of listening to Buddhist focus tapes and an intern from Argentina for Fraga Farm's Rio Santiam cheese to come into being. Located in Sweet Home, Oregon, Fraga Farms is a goat's milk creamery run by Janice Nielson, a former massage therapist and retired naval worker. It is organic, very tuned in to its spiritual side, and named after Neilson's charismatic grandmother in Northern California, who wrote her city asking them to rename a local road surrounding her farm property in her honor.

When Nielson decided she wanted to move beyond the chèvre and farmhouse cheeses she had been making for years, she told an intern that she'd like to learn another style from an international cheesemaker. A month later, Argentine intern Mariano Battro (now owner of La Mariposa Creamery, also in Oregon) walked into her life. He had tons of cheese experience and a Welsh-inspired recipe that his cheesemaker and educator father had specialized in back in Argentina to share.

Rio Santiam is based on that cheese recipe. Named after the Willamette tributary flowing through Sweet Home, this goat's wheel is firm to semifirm, depending on whether it's aged from two to five months. It has a natural, smooth beige and lightly brown-orange rind with a dusting of white mold and a cream-colored center with an occasional hole or crack, and a paste that leans toward a Parmesan's flakiness when older.

When younger, Rio Santiam tastes lively and bright—like grassy crème fraîche. As it ages, it firms up until its paste looks like an extra-aged Manchego, and it takes on a spicy, peppery, brown buttery, sharp bite that makes it perfect for shaving over finished dishes such as bean soups or grilled vegetables.

Nielson stays true to Battro's recipe when she makes Rio. She starts out with raw goat's milk, adds cultures to encourage acidification, and then puts in the rennet. When set, she cuts the curd into quarter-inch cubes, drains some whey, and cooks the curds until they reach "a certain texture" (achieved about forty minutes later). Then she scoops the curds, molds them, and presses them in a hydro press for four hours. When the pH reaches 5.2 (which Nielson helps people remember by telling them it's her height), she brines the wheels for ten hours. Then they're off to the aging room for anywhere from two to five months. While aging, she turns and washes the wheels, to clean them, once a week.

The techniques that Nielson uses are, of course, important to the cheese's final outcome. Just as important, says Nielson, are the mood and intention of the cheesemaker while crafting the cheese.

Nielson said it took her around three years to be able to make cheese successfully and with focus. Balancing all the duties at a creamery—selling at markets, promoting oneself, taking care of the animals, and then actually making the cheese—was overwhelming. She kept getting distracted in the make room. Taking a five-day meditation retreat and listening to Buddhist tapes about how to stay in the present moment and avoid distraction helped her, and her cheese, immensely. Which, no matter what the reader's spiritual persuasion, fares best for us.

"If someone has an attitude, you can definitely taste it in their cheese," says Nielson. "I try to have fun and come at it with purpose. You don't want to be upset when you're making someone's meal. The same goes for cheese."

With its herbal notes, Fraga Farms pairs best with high-acidity lean whites, and high-acidity peppery reds. Nearly any dry, unoaked white will work, from a Chardonnay from Chablis to a Verdejo from Rueda. Reds such as Tempranillos, Bordeaux blends, Gamays, or Northern Italians such as Barbara and Nebbiolo also go well. Heavily oaked wines such as Chardonnays and Zinfandels wouldn't fly with the cheese's acidity. Light to nut brown beers are also a go.

If Fraga's Rio Santiam isn't available near you, some other great aged goat's milk tommes are Impromptu from Andante Dairy in Sonoma, California (pretty rare except in California, and may sometimes also contain cow's milk); Seal Cove Chevrotin from Lamoine, Maine (available on the East Coast and via mail order), and Beltane Farm's Harvest Moon from Lebanon, Connecticut (almost Manchego-esque in style, found on the East Coast and via mail order).

Caproncino, Spinach, and Potatoes

SERVES 2–4

When considering how I wanted a recipe to show off Caproncino's melting ability plus its clean flavors, saag paneer kept popping up in my head. But because, unlike paneer, Capronico melts, I added potatoes for texture. Serve over jasmine rice or wide rice noodles.

1 tablespoon butter
⅓ yellow onion, small dice
½ tablespoon garlic, minced
½ tablespoon ginger, peeled and minced
1 pinch nutmeg, freshly ground
⅛ teaspoon cardamom, ground
¼ teaspoon turmeric, ground
2 small yukon potatoes
½ teaspoon salt
3 cups packed spinach
½ teaspoon freshly squeezed lemon
4 ounces Caproncino, trimmed and small cubed
2–3 tablespoons butter for sautéing, as needed

Bring a medium-sized sauté pan to medium heat. Add the butter and the onion, sauté for 2 minutes. Lower heat to medium-low, add the garlic, ginger, and spices, and stir. Add the potatoes and salt. Cook for 20–30 minutes until the potatoes are tender. Add the spinach, lemon, and cheese and stir until the spinach is wilted. Remove from heat. Serve over rice.

Old Wheels

· · · · ·

The Strong and the Hard

If one was ever to be threatened with cheese, it would be with a Strong and Hard. A gangster, a corrupt politician, or a mom whose kid was just bullied walks into a pub. They see who did them wrong sitting in the center of the room. Right in front of everybody, they saunter over to the culprit, lift their hands above their head, and slam a dry, heavy wheel of Vella Dry Jack or Achandinha's Capricious on the table only inches away from their enemy's face. Necks snap around to see what made the sound like a wooden guillotine crashing into its base. Occasionally the mom or other angry party stabs a pocketknife into the cheese for emphasis, but regardless, the threat is served. These cheeses are serious.

Strong and Hard wheels get to be that way because, one, they're old, and two, they're drier than Death Valley. These wheels could run miles around the youngins in the beginning of the book. They've not only seen cultures and rennet, but experienced plenty of heat, been squished and stacked until the whey was scared out of them, and been banished to a cellar for seven months to two years.

One intention of putting these wheels through the ringer is to make them less perishable. The cultures that created the inspirations for most of these dry cheeses, such as those of the Parmesan Reggiano area, wanted a dry cheese that would last. If they squeezed most of the moisture out of the wheels through pressing and more whey was lost through aging, the result was a cheese that could be eaten over months or years. No need to worry about these guys getting moldy or stinky like a freshie left out for a week.

As the cheeses aged, they became saltier as the moisture evaporated. The taste also became more concentrated, or so altered that they introduced entire new flavor levels (hello, umami). This made them especially potent cheeses when grated or shaved over pasta or gratins. A little of these cheeses goes a long way, whether on a cheese board or in lasagna.

Some American Strong and Hards were created in imitation of European cheeses when the original was unavailable, such as Vella for Parmesan. Others, such as Valley Shepherd's Perlitta, were created to show that although the originals (Mimolette) are delicious, they could be upped by twisting tradition. Others were just created for creation's sake. Whatever the reason they were made here, American Strong and Hards always hold their own. They're not as easy to find as the original Euros because they're so labor intensive to produce, but they're worth seeking out.

Vella Dry Jack, California

When Italians get far enough from home that their trusted daily dairy, drink, or caffeine staples aren't readily available, sometimes a green plastic can of processed cheese hits the fan. With the speed of a gnocchi master rolling a batch of potato dumplings, either an importing business is set up, stat, or someone creates a culinary substitute. Such is the case with Vella Dry Jack.

Around nine pounds and three inches high, the dense, aged, and pressed cheese has a pleated rind the color of dark chocolate and a center the hue of melted butter. Aged from eight months for the standard Dry selection, to three years for the Golden Bear Select, Vella Dry Jack is nutty and blessed with beefy flavors reminiscent of a seared rib eye. Just like its uncle Parmesan Reggiano, it, too, likes to be grated over a plate of pasta with peppery olive oil as much as it loves a plate of artisan salami and olives.

Like sixty other creameries around 1915, the Vellas knew when cheese wholesaler D. F. DeBernardi unveiled a really old wheel of Monterey Jack (a semisoft, mild, cow's milk melting cheese) from storage that he had something special. To an Italian American population aching for a former kitchen staple, the cheese tasted a lot like Parmesan. And it was a hell of a lot cheaper. Everyone hopped on board.

Now, Vella is one of the last three remaining creameries of the original sixty that rode the Dry Jack wave high before Italian imports slowed during World World II and Americans started favoring fresh cheese. And even though it's one of the few union-operated cheese shops in the nation (and a proud one at that), Vella is still family owned.

The patriarch, Ig Vella, who passed away just before this book was written, saw to it that they make their Dry Jack exactly the way they did in the early 1900s. They're champions for traditional American cheesemaking. Unlike many guys who went under in the thirties, Vella never tried to amp up production by using skim milk so the wheels would dry faster. When new food safety regulations tried to mandate switching from wood to plastic cheese aging boards, Ig's father, Tom Vella, went to Washington, DC, and lobbied until the law let him keep his old wooden bakery boards, which he had been using for years.

Everything that they do at Vella—from using "four or so water jugs" to press the freshly formed wheels still wrapped in cheesecloth overnight, to using a salt brine that they change "right about the time that the tank starts to leak," says a Vella cheesemaker Roger Rannikar, to cure the wheels for three days—screams old school.

But they also set traditions. Tired of lampblack (carbon soot originally used to coat Parm rinds), the Vellas switched to coating their rind with cocoa powder, pepper, and oil in 1936. The oil preserved the wheels, the cocoa kept the oil suspended so the cheese could breathe, and the pepper kept the bugs away prior to refrigeration.

It's this coating that Vella "newbies"—new workers who haven't advanced to milk pasteurization or cheesemaking, Rannikar explains—are assigned to hand-rub on the wheels after they've dried on racks for three days. Once the cocoa's on the Dry Jack, no one's to touch, flip, or spin the wheels. They join the other 30,000 wheels maturing in the aging room.

Housed in the original, stone-walled cheese plant, a former brewhouse shut down during Prohibition turned failed mushroom business, Vella continues to share their tradition today with Sonoma locals, visiting tourists, and a plastic Santa Claus waving from the third-floor window. Vella is a cultural historical institution that speaks to the pleasures of sitting at a table with friends, cheese, and glass of Sangiovese. This Dry Jack can be found in many specialty shops, and ordered directly from anywhere in the nation. If eager to try others, seek out Spring Hill's from Petaluma, California (made from Jersey cow's milk); or Rumiano Cheese's from Crescent City, Calfornia (both aforementioned available around California and via mail order).

Achandinha Capricious, California

My mother used to tell me a fable about a little boy who tricked a giant into thinking he was so powerful he could squeeze water from a stone. A bright young lad to realize the power of dairy at such a young age, the child switched a stone for a wheel of cheese when the monster wasn't looking, and squeezed it until it dripped with whey. The giant, who thought the whey was water, was so impressed with the boy's strength that he agreed to leave the boy's people alone.

I'm pretty sure that Achandinha's Capricious was the noble cheese that fooled the giant. Hard, round, and flat like a stone with smooth edges, dry and crumbly with a dusty brown and orange rind like the Grand Canyon, Capricious evokes a time when cheesemakers didn't aim for homogenous wheels, or cater to mild tastes. Peppery, herbal, lemony, grassy, meaty, and with a blue sharpness that grows stronger with age, Capricious is a cheese that stands alone.

Achadinha Capricious

Somewhat similar to Vella Dry Jack in production, Achandinha is also pressed in cheesecloth during production and aged for at least seven to eight months. But that's where the similarities end. Where Vella concentrates on crafting a consistent cow's milk cheese to meet community needs, Achandinha works with the more variable milk of their own goat herd to create a cheese that doesn't shy away from being punchier from one batch to the next, or letting ambient molds dictate the rind or the flavor.

The Pachecos aren't concerned with following a straight path.

Third-generation cow farmers exhausted from dealing with fluctuating milk market prices and the environmental erosion that cattle inflict on land, the Pachecos shocked their Sonoma neighbors and bought a folding goat cheese company. Convinced that goats would pave their future path, they sold most of their cows, learned goat husbandry, and decided to make cheese.

Although chèvre or a Loire Valley crottin style might have been an easier and quicker sell than a punchy, dry goat's milk wheel, cheesemaker Donna set her sights on the sassy, good-hearted, yet occasionally foul-mouthed-type cheese that dares you to love it while showing you its tattoos.

Luckily, Donna, Pacheco matriarch and Achandinha cheesemaker, has cheesemaking apprentices to help her manage Capricious—her eighteen-year-old son, William, and occasionally her thirteen-year-old son, Daniel. They are a true family farm, as exemplified by one son playfully splashing his mother with cheese curds while they're draining off the whey and an occasional "You watch your mouth" when another gets descriptive with the vat temperature.

To make Capricious, they start by pasteurizing the milk, adding rennet and starters, then lightly cooking and stirring the curd (which takes way too long if you ask the son stirring the paddle while trying to locate his favorite country song on the iPod). Next, they salt the curd, stirring it with their hands so the curds don't release too much liquid before their time (goat cheese has less butterfat than cow's and goat's milk, so they want to preserve the moisture as long as possible).

Then, they wet down the cheesecloth with whey to properly acidify the material and scoop the curd into about fifty cheesecloths in a practice called "lumping." Now the family puts their body weight into it. Spinning, squashing, and slapping the filled cloth against the side of the vat, Donna leans over the vat in her vintage plastic flowered apron, pressing even more whey from the solidifying curds.

The cheesecloth curds head to a press, where they're pressed with their own weight. When sufficiently dry, they're moved to a cheese room, where they're stamped with a date (Daniel's favorite job) and rubbed with olive oil to prevent moisture loss from the now whey-depleted goat cheese.

Around eight months later, the Capricious are ready to come out and play. Whether grated over freshly shelled fava beans or roasted peaches with honey, Capricious is a great food finisher. It also shines as a lone starter on a cheese plate with figs and a dry Riesling with enough oomph to handle its spunk, or as a dessert with blackberry flower honey and a sweet Riesling. A couple other firm, drier goat's milk cheeses to try are Blue Ledge's Riley's Coat (not quite as strong, available in the East Coast and through mail order) from Salsbury, Vermont; and Birchrun Hill's Clipper (very concentrated flavors, available mainly on the East Coast) from Chester Springs, Pennsylvania.

Valley Shepherd Perlitta, New Jersey

Located on 120 acres in the suburbs of Long Valley, New Jersey, Valley Shepherd Creamery is a rare cheese bird. A creamery, cheese distributer, grass-fed meat and pasta company, education center, seller of lamb's wool blankets and Ewe-Poo, Valley Shepherd has more facets to its business than the *Star Wars* space opera enterprise. The action figures will come later.

Former engineers and developers Eran Wajswol and his wife, Debra, make Perlitta—likely the most aged sheep's milk commercially available in the country. And I say "available" as if I were talking about that attractive, kind, wealthy, recently widowed neurosurgeon whose text messages are packed with female offers of shoulders to lean on.

Like many of the Strong and Hards, Perlitta is in very short supply, but I couldn't resist including it here. I'm hoping that cheese lovers will fall in love with aged sheep's milk cheeses and be willing to pay a little extra for their deliciousness so cheesemakers are able invest the time and extra labor it takes to make more wheels for you and me, so we can always find them.

Perlitta is an aged, raw sheep's and Jersey cow's milk cheese blend made in the fashion of France's Mimolette. It is one pound and has a hard, rough rind that looks like tightly grained cantaloupe skin. Naturally dyed with annatto seed, its center is hued orange like an autumn leaf.

It looks like Mimolette, but it tastes different in many ways. It has the Frenchie's caramelly, slightly sweet flavor, but Perlitta also tastes a little beefier, like brown butter, and it finishes with a very sharp, welcoming bite. Its texture is different, too. Instead of slicing in shards, Valley Shepherd's extra aged slices smoothly, with a few crumbles.

Perlitta takes two years to come into maturation. It's the make, says cheesemaker Eran, that's simple. Cultures and rennet are added to raw sheep's and cow's milk. So is annatto (cheesemakers in France originally added this natural orange-colored seed dye to Mimolette because Louis XIV wanted a cheese the hue of Edam). When the curd is ready, it's cut, the curds are "washed" with warm water to remove some lactose and reduce acidity and sharpness development, and then stirred for an hour on low heat. Then they increase the temperature a bit to cook the curds for an hour or so.

Next, they scoop the curds into five-pound molds and drain whey for half an hour. Then the molds are sent to a machine that presses forty wheels at one time to remove more whey. But there's more draining to come. If a cheese is to age for two years, most of the moisture must be leeched to inhibit bad bacteria growth and off flavors. So Perlitta also hangs out overnight to drain. In the morning it's sent to brine for two days, then to the aging area, where it's turned daily for three days. After being flipped, Perlitta is set on ash wood shelves and left for cheese mites.

Cheese mites are what give Mimolette and Perlitta their cantaloupe rind. When the little cheese lovers get hungry, they nibble on cheese rinds, hence the textured rind. This is a good thing, in Eran's mind. "They call them *petite amies* in France," says Eran. "They're part of cheesemaking like the mold that makes Brie and the blue that makes blues blue." Eran puts the wheels in a wetter area of cheese cave, which the mites like. When there, they leave the other wheels, whose rinds Eran doesn't want to look so textured, alone. Then Perlitta sits with its newfound friends for two years.

The Wajswols tell visitors on their farm tours and in their sold-out cheesemaking classes about how much work and time goes into Perlitta and other cheesemaking endeavors. By focusing on education and situating themselves in a suburban area like New Jersey, Valley Shepherd has not only made self-distribution easier, but helped facilitate farm visits from the surrounding communities such as New

York City. Experiencing it firsthand is the only way, says Eran, that people understand what they're paying for and see how important it is to support farmers, cheesemakers, and the stores that carry artisan American cheeses.

"People need an education about what they can have and why they pay to support us," says Eran.

If you can get your hands on an aged Perlitta, booze it up. It loves harder alcohols and beers. As mentioned earlier, Perlitta's got a bite, so its sharpness needs some assuaging. Dark stouts and brown ales work well, as do bourbons and scotch. Richer reds with a bit of residual sugar, such as Zinfandels or Shirazes, fit, too, and stickies such as port and sherries.

Try these other aged sheep's milk cheeses if Perlitta proves to be as difficult to find as it might—they're not colored with annatto and, depending on their age, will likely be less sharp: Bonnieview Farm's Ben Nevis (try this one when it's aged five or more months, available on the East Coast and via mail order) from Craftsbury, Vermont; and Wisconsin Sheep Milk Dairy Co-op's Dante (aged, but still lighter in taste than Perlitta, found nationwide) from River Falls, Wisconsin.

Perlitta Meatballs

MAKES 35–45 MEATBALLS

Take away the traditional breadcrumbs and there's room for the aged, earthy, buttery, sharp Perlitta to make its mark. I love the butteriness Perlitta provides these balls, but any "hard and strong" cheese may be substituted with great results. You could also try a mix of beef and pork, but I think using a little more strongly flavored lamb pairs better with the earthy cheese. Don't use lean meat, and don't skip the tester step. It's hard to add more seasoning to the meatballs after the fact. Meatballs may be seared and refrigerated up to four hours before serving (bring to room temperature before baking).

½ pound ground lamb
1 pound ground pork
2 garlic cloves, minced
½ yellow onion, finely chopped
1 egg, beaten
½ cup parsley, chopped
4 sage leaves, finely chopped
⅛ teaspoon nutmeg, freshly ground
1½ teaspoon salt
4 ounces grated Perlitta
1 cup rice or white wheat flour for dredging
2–5 tablespoons olive oil for frying

Add all ingredients but the dredging flour and frying oil to a large bowl and mix thoroughly with your hands.

Take 1–2 tablespoons of the mix from the bowl, roll into a ball, dredge in flour, then flatten between your palms. This will be your tester ball. Bring a large sauté pan to medium-high heat. Add 1 tablespoon of oil. Once the oil is hot, quickly fry the tester, cool, then taste. If you'd like the ball with more salt or pepper, add more to the original meat mix.

When seasoned to your liking, form the balls by shaping 2–2½ tablespoons into oblong circles. The oblong shape makes them easier to sear and quicker to bake. Place on a baking sheet.

Put dredging flour on a plate. Lightly roll each ball in the flour and return to the baking sheet.

Preheat oven to 350 degrees.

Bring the large sauté pan you used for your test run again to medium-high heat. Add 1½ tablespoons of oil. Once the oil is hot, start searing the balls in batches for 5–7 minutes or until the seared sides are a golden-medium brown, flipping only once. Do not overcrowd the pan—leave each ball with ¾–1 inch of personal space or you'll end up steaming rather than searing the balls. When seared, move to a fresh baking sheet. When ready to serve, finish baking for 7–10 minutes in the oven, until the center is thoroughly cooked.

Washed and Smeared Rinds

· · · · ·

What the Hell Is Going On
in the Kitchen?

At the end of the day, the pervading scent gracing the clothes and body of even the most careful cheesemonger is most likely a washed rind. This powerful aroma requires the wearer to undergo a full showering before first and second dates and sometimes an explanation to scent-sensitive people they might be sitting next to on the subway.

Washed rind cheeses are stuff of stinky, delicious legends. Époisses and Forsterkäse are good European examples. They start out smelling sweet when young, then, after being wrapped in paper or plastic for a few days, gain a sultriness that could match Kathleen Turner's voice. They smell like sweet, imperfect love—like a couple that's so enamored with each other that smelling their partner's workout T-shirts when they're off on a business trip warms their heart.

There's a reason for that. Soft washed rinds are ripe with *Brevibacterium linens.* This is a good bacteria that keeps the bad bacteria out, and it's also what provides the strong smell. This bacteria can also be found on more stinky stuff than cheese (like that aforementioned T-shirt).

It is widely suggested that washed rinds were first made by monks—as early as the seventh century in France. Monks had large supplies of alcohol and time on their hands, and mixed the two. The story goes that after noticing the rinds of the cheeses they were making cracking in the cellar, they tried rubbing them with alcohol brine solutions. The result was a strong-smelling, yet surprisingly sweet cheese that stood in for meat when they were fasting.

There are two types of washed rinds: There are the hard ones, such as those made in the Alpine regions that are rubbed down with a mainly saltwater brine and take on *B. linens* mostly through ambient means. Then there are the washed rinds, called smeared rinds by many Midwestern cheesemakers such as Wisconsin's Myron Olson of Chalet Cheese, that we're discussing here. The curds of these washed and smeared cheeses are kept large so they stay moist and their softness is encouraged through a *B. linens* or a brine–alcohol–*B. linens* application that breaks down their fat and protein structure, says Olson. Some don't need the extra *B. linens* boost in the brine, but most do.

One of the first washed rinds to compel Americans was Limburger (it's in this book's "American Originals and Inspirations" category). While it's not as popular as it once was when the Belgian and German cheese had its crew of folks who were accustomed to its strong scents, it has a steady following. Washed rind cheeses in general are gaining popularity as people become accustomed to (or re-familiarize themselves with) the natural scents and tastes that come with the artisan cheese world. The artisan cheese revolution will not be defunkified.

Von Trapp Farmstead Oma, Vermont

Despite having to wake up at four in the morning to milk the cows, then tend to the animals' and farm's every other need, then do it all again in the evening, there are some who wake up every day on a dairy farm knowing that there's little else they'd rather do with their life. Sebastian and Dan von Trapp's grandparents decided this in their forties and moved their five kids to Vermont to start a dairy farm. The third-generation Von Trapp brothers—eh, not so much.

They flew the dairy coop. They got jobs in software engineering and liked to believe their future careers wouldn't involve milking heifers when most people in the nation were sleeping. But when small dairy farms around their childhood home started disappearing because farmers couldn't break even on milk prices, the brothers returned home. They helped their family transition to organic farming so they'd be in a different milk market and started making Oma so they'd be able to control where some of their milk went.

Oma, which is German for "grandmother," is named in honor of the brothers' Austrian grandmother and activist who bought the family farm. It seems the boys have come to terms with their birthright. A sturdy, soft square just over a pound and a half and about six inches in diameter, this cheese has a thin, firm, edible orange rind and a center the color of vanilla custard.

Oma is made with raw cow's milk, and its rind lets off a funky whiff when the paper is unwrapped. Inside, however, it's all sweet, buttery, and just a little earthy (good for funk novices), and its texture ranges from semisoft and a little wiggly to custardy and bouncy.

This proud cheese with a delicate washed rind was almost a Camembert-style cheese with a white, bloomy rind and mushroomy, soft center. What kept us from almost missing out on of one of the best funk mistresses around was that the brothers wanted to use raw milk and they couldn't get a Camembert-style bloomy rind to age past sixty days—the amount of time legally required to age a raw milk cheese sold in the United States. Because keeping it raw, says Sebastian, allows them "to capture everything we can from the milk we have, all the complexity," the brothers decided on making a Reblochon-inspired style instead with a firmer consistency and a washed rind.

The milk for Oma goes straight to the cheese vat, where it's warmed to ripening temperature to activate the cultures. Rennet is added, the curd set, and then it is cut into walnut-sized pieces. They quickly heat and stir the milk, then pour the curds from an elevated vat into block forms on trays. At this point the mixture that goes into the forms is about one-third the mass of the original milk in the vat (still a lot of moisture).

After the curds go in trays, they are flipped ten to fifteen minutes after molding and then again another three to four times that day. The next day they get a long five-hour saltwater bath in the brine tanks. Then each batch is set on its own wire rack and wheeled to the cellar. A week later they're sent to the Cellars at Jasper Hill in neighboring Greensboro, Vermont (profiled in "Blue: No, No, It's a Good Pain," page 179), where they get their orange coats. Jasper Hill washes them down with a saltwater brine that's been blessed by ambient yeasts and our washed rind friend, *Brevibacterium linens.* They stay there until they hit the sixty-day mark and are sent off to loving cheese shops and homes.

When at home, Sebastian eats Oma with beer. Pretty much any craft type, he says, but Belgian ales are his favorite with this cheese. I agree with his beer inspiration, and also like Oma with sweeter, aromatic white wines such as off-dry Rieslings and Gewürztraminers. But Oma is as great cooked as it is on a cheese plate. Sebastian likes his on a fried egg or melted on broccoli and raves about the pizzas at Roberta's in Brooklyn, who proved him wrong about Oma being too strong to top a pie.

Oma is available around the country in limited quantities, but if you can't pin this strong beauty down, try Birchrun Hills Red Cat from Chester Springs, Pennsylvania (mainly East Coast allocated); Hook's Stinky Fotene, made in Mineral Point, Wisconsin (found mainly in the Midwest but available through mail order); and Cato Corner's Hooligan from Colchester, Connecticut (available on the East Coast and through mail order).

Rivers Edge Chèvre Mayor of Nye Beach, Oregon

Normally when someone tells me, "I love cheese," I nod my head and smile. Yes, me, too. But when the daughter of a mother-daughter

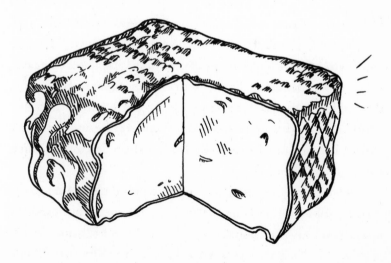

Mayor of Nye Beach

cheesemaking team says it right after aiming her rifle at a distant coyote threatening her milking goats, it holds special meaning.

Rivers Edge's Patricia and Astraea Morford live in the grand European cheesemaking tradition on the second floor of their house, which rests atop their dairy in Logsden, a town on the Oregon coast. There they make more than twenty-eight cheeses, one of the many beauties being Mayor of Nye Beach.

Mayor of Nye Beach is a washed rind goat's milk cheese made with the milk from the team's single herd. It's named after a vocal man who titles himself mayor of his local Nye Beach. A square about three inches high and wide, its rind is chanterelle mushroom orange.

Beneath the rind the cheese has a slim pearlescent layer. The layer edges toward the cheese's center, which starts out semifirm and crumbly and softens slightly as it ripens. Not only is Mayor's rind the color of a chanterelle mushroom, but the cheese tastes like the lightly sautéed fungus, too. Want more? Add a sweet oyster plucked straight from the sea squeezed with a sliced lemon. This is one dynamic little cube.

Mayor of Nye Beach is one of the rare softer washed rind goat cheeses in the United States. It's a category that's growing, but still dominated by cow's milk cheeses. Sheep's milk versions are even rarer. Add a strong washed rind scent to the vibrant flavor of goat's milk, and you have a combo that's yet to be fully appreciated in the States. Yet take a ripe Mayor out for an hour before serving and put it on a cheese plate next to a dish of honey and be prepared to witness minds shifting.

The vibrant square starts out with pasteurized milk. After Rivers Edge's goats are milked and the milk's transferred to the creamery and pasteurized, the cheesmakers add a proprietary blend of three cultures to it. Then the mix is allowed to rest for around half an hour.

Next, rennet is stirred in and allowed to sit for about forty-five minutes until the curd is set.

Patricia and Astraea both use scientific measurements from time to time as the process goes along—pH readers and the such—but they generally make cheese by feel. Patricia grew up with goats, bought her own herd in 1970, raised her children and grandchild on goat's milk, learned how to make cheese via taking classes and reading books, then licensed Rivers Edge in 2005. Astraea has never taken any classes in her craft, she learned it entirely from her mother (who, if Astraea's skills say anything, is also a good shot), and the couple prides themselves on being able to track the cheese's progress via taste, touch, feel, and smell.

"People have been making cheese for hundreds of years in dirt-floored huts," says Patricia. "If we can't make it with what we got, well, that's pretty sad."

After they intuit that the curd is cut-worthy, the duo slices it into one-inch or so curds. Then they heat, stir, and cook the curds a bit to help keep them firm and moist. Next, they dispel some of the whey, add warm water, and rinse the curds as is done with Gouda to remove some of the lactic acid.

Then the Mayor curds are poured into square forms and flipped so moisture is evenly dispersed. The next day they're salted and put away to age. As the rind grows orange, the cheese is rubbed several times with a mixture of salt and local Rogue Brewery's Dead Guy Ale in Newport, Oregon.

It's no surprise that the cheesemaking duo wouldn't shy away from a genre of cheese that has yet to earn as many fans at home as a cow's milk washed rind. They have mastered more cheese styles than Prince has made albums and do it all while running their dairy, caring for chickens and a family garden, and protecting their goats from predators. They seem ready to take on anything but those damn deer trying to eat Astraea's cabbages.

A cheese this dynamic calls for a white wine with little distraction and plenty of acid. Pour with a Melon de Bourgone from the Muscadet region of France, Roero Arneis, Tocai Fruiliano, Gruner Vetliner, dry Riesling, or a sweet Loire Valley Chenin Blanc. Wit beers love Mayor, too, as do gin or vodka cocktails with a splash of elderflower syrup or lychee juice. Several other goat cheese washed rinds to try are Capriole's Mont St. Francis from Greenville, Indiana (available nationwide and by mail order); Haystack Mountain's Red Cloud from Longmont, Colorado (sporadically found nationwide); and Redwood Hill's Gravenstein Gold from Sebastopol, California (West Coast–focused).

Meadow Creek Grayson, Virginia

Dairy farmers for twenty-three years before making Grayson, Helen and Rick Feete of Meadow Creek looked all over Virginia before settling on the ideal spot for their new creamery. They found a place twenty-eight hundred feet above sea level in the Appalachian Mountains. Cows would love it, they thought, plus it was only three hours away from Harrison, a string band mecca where they could go clogging when they needed to let off some steam.

Though the banjo and classical guitar–playing couple don't head to Harrison much anymore since, as Helen puts it, "It was a lot easier back then to stay up all night and go milking in the morning," they're still just as in love with Grayson County. The land is picturesque and the area's elevation makes for a unique climate and vegetation for their cows. Lots of deep-rooted, mineral-rich grasses such as rye keep the cows happy and grazing from April to December—the only time when the Feetes make Grayson.

Grayson, a thick-rinded soft square, is one of the sweetest stinkers around. And as does a French mother when she calls her child her *"petit chou"* (little cabbage), I say "stinker" with the upmost respect and adoration.

The hue of Grayson's thick, edible rind is between the color of a fillet of wild-caught salmon and a tangerine. Beneath the rind, its soft, shiny paste looks like a crème brûlée with an extra egg yolk mixed in. It slices like Tallegio, and just like the Lombardian washed rind, Grayson would taste fantastic melted on a pizza or over polenta, too.

The first thing that hits you when unwrapping Grayson is the scent. It goes from light, airy, and a little pungent when young, to downright funky after it's been sitting on a store shelf for a couple weeks, like that box of dusty James Brown LPs in Uncle Larry's basement. Its taste, however, is a lot subtler than its aroma suggests. Same goes for most washed rinds. A Grayson bite reveals flavors of caramelized onions and chives, beef, fresh cream, and sweet butter.

The making of the four-pound Grayson is an homage to washed rinds everywhere. Helen cites Durrus, the cheese named after the Irish town of the same name, as her main inspiration, but the Feetes list everything from Italy's Tallegio to France's Livarot as their influences.

The two mixed and matched techniques and recipes until they created a cheese they liked. Then, they had to figure out how to age the raw milk cheese to sixty days without producing off flavors or having rind issues. They had a long learning curve, what Helen calls "a three-to-four-year struggle," until they got their new cellar and mastered their technique.

Most of the flavor develops in the cellars, says Helen, but of course, one always starts with the curds. The Feetes' morning milk is pumped straight to the tank, to which cultures and rennet are added to ripen and then coagulate the milk. The curd is cut into pea-sized pieces and cooked very quickly at a temperature two to three degrees higher. Next the curds are molded, flipped about three times, then set aside until they're brined the next day.

Then it's rind time. After brining, the rinds are left to dry for a couple days before the cheese hits the cellar, where it's washed with a *Brevibacterium linens*–saltwater solution. As Grayson sits in the cellar with its wet rind exposed, different bacteria, molds, and yeasts stop by for a visit. They give the cheese its funky-sweet character and orange hue, and make the cheese soft. As the cheese is flipped, handled, and washed down about twice a week over the next sixty days, its rind grows thicker and firmer. They slow down the washing right before shipping.

Once you get Grayson out of the shop and into your kitchen, you'll find it very adaptable. Helen loves it at room temperature with Virginia country ham, bacon, or dates or dried figs. I'd be up for a plate full of such goodies or with pickled vegetables and onions, and I also like the cheese warmed. It becomes a sweet, creamy, saucy cheese when heated. It's great melted over pizza, polenta, or in a panini with mustard and arugula. While it's a master in the kitchen or on the cheese board, it's a little pickier with alcohol. Go with something with a hint of sweetness—such as a Kabinett or Spatlese level Riesling, a Gewürztraminer, or a Belgian tripel.

Other great Livarot- and Tallegio-inspired washed rinds to try are Nicasio's Nicasio Sqaure from Marin, California (distributed somewhat widely); and Lazy Lady's Barick Obama from Westfield, Vermont (East Coast–centric).

Mayor of Nye Beach Crisped Rice Treats

MAKES AROUND 10 SQUARES

Sometimes strong-smelling, but always sweet-tasting, washed rind cheeses are perfect dessert material. Here, slices of Mayor of Nye Beach top a twist on the classic crisped rice and marshmallow treat. Lemon zest highlights the fresh lemon flavors in the cheeses, and brown butter and brown rice cereal keep the dessert from tasting too sweet. If you don't have brown rice cereal near you, just go with the normal variety.

> 3 tablespoons butter
> 20 regular-sized marshmallows
> 3 cups crisped brown rice cereal
> zest of one lemon
> 10 ounces Mayor of Nye Beach, at room
> temperature

Place the butter in a large saucepan and bring to medium heat. Shake the pan to melt the butter evenly. Once the butter melts, it will start to foam. At this point, stir the butter constantly with a wooden spoon for about 2 minutes until the butter deposits on the bottom of the pan are light hazelnut brown.

Add the marshmallows to the pan and stir until melted and free from lumps. Turn off the heat. Pour the crisped rice cereal and lemon zest into the saucepan and stir until all is the same consistency.

Pour into a buttered pan and press the mixture down evenly either with lightly buttered hands, a spatula, or wax paper. After cooling, cut into squares. Top each square with a 1-ounce slice of Mayor of Nye Beach.

Blue

· · · · ·

No, No, It's a Good Pain

I'd give it some good thought before entering a serious relationship with someone who doesn't like blue cheese. How a person feels about the veined ones says a lot about them. More than an expression of taste, a love for blues is a declaration that one is open to experiencing a little pain, that one could face adversity and work through the initial surprise and find the joy in strife, or at least in fermented milk. Not that I haven't dated some doozies who loved Point Reyes crumbles.

A love for blue says a lot because, let's face it, not all blue cheeses are easy to like. Some sting a little or are tangy. Some have a strong scent. Some look funny. Others are sweet like candy, and as comforting as a pat of salted butter on warm bread.

The realm of blue cheese is still growing in the United States. The good ones are smaller in number than other styles. It's not just that it's a learned taste (though watching a French child bite into a Roquefort wedge as if it were a slice of cake suggests otherwise), or that most cheesemakers would rather make cheeses that are loved unconditionally like a double crème might be. It's also that many cheesemakers hesitate to get involved with a cheese whose spores jump all over the other wheels in the cellar. Making blue requires a lot of space and discipline.

Out of those that have made it in here, British blues like Stilton and Roquefort are the most common blue inspirations. Cheesemakers often visit the regions for inspiration (and some claim to scrape the sides of the Roquefort caves to snag the original molds). They're the standards, the classics to which traditionalists look for inspiration. Not all are traditionalists, though, and blue is a genre where people like to play around, too. Spores here, spores there, spores everywhere—these days blue cheese veins can be found in everything from cheddars to bloomy rind goat cheeses. There are as many blue tastes as there are places where Dr. Seuss would eat green eggs and ham.

So there's no reason why everyone shouldn't be able to find a blue of his or her own to love and hold. They're worth the effort.

Jasper Hill Bayley Hazen Blue, Vermont

It's rare that a cheesemaker's final wheel is the exact one they intended to make when they first installed their milk vat. A cheese is, as Jasper Hill's cheesemaker Mateo Kehler puts it, an evolution. It's about seeing where nature, the reality of a dairy person's and cheesemaker's life, and an idea converge. The final product—the finished cheese—is the result of many adjustments, surprise inspirations, accidents, and even personal habits, as is Jasper Hill's Bayley Hazen Blue.

Bayley Hazen reaches ten inches high and is covered in a thin, sturdy soft orange and brown rind that keeps the cheese's center firm and drier than most blues—no cheese water leaking here. Though very similar texturally to Stilton in that it crumbles and slices neatly, the heavily blue-mold-ridden center is nearly as mild as a Danish blue.

As Mateo Kehler puts it, Bayley is "a gateway into a whole other cheese realm." It's a gentle, starter blue that in its subtlety helps to welcome novices into the blue cheese world but still impresses with its layered nuances. Sweet and salty, it tastes like fresh cream and oyster mushrooms sautéed in brown butter and hazelnuts.

Modeled after Devon Blue from Ticklemore in Devon, England, Bayley Hazen came to be through a series of fortunes. Kehler trained for two years in England's cheese industry and fell in love with their blues. Then he interned with someone who created a unique blue recipe and adapted it to his needs. Finally, he decided to make Bayley Hazen in a rare natural-rinded style so it would stand out among the many blues in the United States. Stand out it does.

To make Bayley Hazen, Kehler starts out with raw cow's milk from the Kehler family's herd (taken care of by his brother and Jasper Hill co-owner Andy Kehler), to which he adds *Penicillium roqueforti* spores, enzymes, and cultures. Rennet is added after an hour and left to set, and then curds are cut into grape-sized pieces. Proof that the cheese and the cheesemaker have equal influence on each other in creating a final product, Ticklemore's Robin Congden created the Devon Blue method so he would have time to take many smoke breaks. Instead of stirring the curds continuously as is done with most blues, Congden stirs, lets the curds rest for twenty minutes, then repeats around five times. While outside lighting up (Congden, not Kehler, who says Jasper Hill is "working on a full-blown wellness program"), the curds form skins. These curd skins have a big part in making Bayley Hazen different.

After the pH drops off in the curds, and everything "feels right," Kehler pulls the curds and molds them. This is when the curd skins get to work. The molds are turned twice a day for four days, salted, then cellared. While the curds are settling, the skins keep the curds from completely binding together and they act as a barrier to keep the curds from collapsing into one another.

Although binding cheese curds is normally good because it creates a smooth, tight paste, a looser paste is generally desired with blue cheese so oxygen has room to circulate in the crevices. That's when it can interact with the classic blue *Penicillium roqueforti* that it has been inoculated with and turn it blue. The skins make even more space for the *P. roqueforti* to circulate. After Bayley has sat in the cellar for seven to eight days, it's also pierced with a stainless steel fork, allowing more air to circulate. Piercing holes in blues is how blue-veined cheeses get veined. But it's mainly the curd skins that make Bayley Hazen a healthy, blue-veined playground.

As all this blue-ing action is going on, an edible natural rind forms in the cellar over the next three weeks. Most blues, such as Maytag and Point Reyes, or even Devon, are wrapped with aluminum foil to inhibit a natural rind once the interior blue has developed. Not Bayley Hazen. Kehler prides the cheese on the nutty dimension the rind adds to the blue and lets it age at cellar temperatures rather than in the near refrigerator-like conditions that many others do, because it encourages the rind and lets the cheese mellow out a bit. This cheese may be one of the most studied of all in the country. As of this writing, Harvard scientists are mapping out the succession of yeast, molds, and enzymes that add to its flavor. It's a scientific and natural wonder.

What to pair with such a wonder? I avoid reds, leaning toward white dessert wines like a late-harvest Chenin Blanc from France's Loire Valley, ice wines, sweeter sherries and Madeiras, or Rieslings from Germany of Spatlese level or higher sugar level. Mateo Kehler prefers barley wine, Belgian tripels, quads or oatmeal stouts. Or he keeps it simple and beer-free, drizzling honey over Bayley spread on toast, or heating it up in a grilled cheese sandwich with bacon and red onion chutney.

Some other good natural-rinded blues to try are Clover Creek's Pirate Blue in Morrison's Cove, Pennsylvania (subtle, from the milk of five different cow breeds, available on the East Coast and in limited supply around the country); Blackberry Farm's Blackberry Blue from Walland, Tennessee (subtle, earthy, available via mail order nationwide); and Bonnieview Farm's Mossend Blue from Craftsbury Common, Vermont (buttery, firm, available in East Coast shops and via mail order). Two non-natural-rinded favorites, widely available nationwide, are Point Reyes Blue from Point Reyes, California; and Hidden Spring's Bohemian Blue from Westby, Wisconsin.

Roelli Dunbarton Blue, Wisconsin

Even though it's snuggled in the blue section of this book, Dunbarton Blue isn't really just a blue any more than Cornwell West is "just an academic." It's more multifaceted. Dunbarton is a rare cheese unicorn. A blue-cheddar hybrid, it has the power to ease novices into the veined world, add another level to a cheddar lover's sturdy home, and blow away anyone who thought that cheese categories were stagnant.

An expert blend of two of the best cheese styles in the world—cheddar and blue—Dunbarton Blue demonstrates the breadth of possibilities for a cheesemaker wanting to create something original from the tried-and-true tools they have in their cheese toolbox.

From the outside, Dunbarton Blue looks like brain lobes from my biological anthropology coloring book. Its curds, which are kept large when cut, leave little "lobe" gaps when settling during aging. Inside, the paste ranges from golden to buttery depending on whether made with summer milk or winter milk. Dispersed in the semifirm, slightly crumbly cheese are blue veins running up and down the cheese's backbone.

The taste is halfway between a bandaged-wrapped cheddar with a kick such as Lincolnshire Poacher from Somerset, England, and a buttery, salty Stilton. It crumbles in the mouth like an older cheddar but the *Penicillium roqueforti* pumping through the wheel's veins reminds you of what you're really dealing with. Earthy, buttery, mushroomy like a portabello, it's a salt-of-the-earth-type cheese, one that Grams and Pops would be proud of, even if they never would have dared to make it themselves.

Cheesemaker Chris Roelli's family did make cheese before him—but nothing like this. Swiss immigrants of the 1900s, Roelli's family settled in the rolling hills of Green County, Wisconsin, partially because it reminded them of Switzerland, and partially because, Roelli says, a friend who went to check out Russia first told them they had better pack a gun. They decided to go west instead. Originally a dairy family, the Roellis quickly settled in and proceeded to make commodity cheese until 1991, when the pressures of a bad milk market led them to close the plant.

After the closing, they set up a milk hauling and farm equipment business. Yet third-generation dairy farmer Chris Roelli's cheese fire was still alive. He headed back to school for cheesemaking and fulfilled the licensing hours required under state law. Then he started selling the favorite Wisconsin delicacy—cheese curds—from a rolling cheese factory (a milk-hauling truck) that he called "Cheese on Wheels" to build a little cash flow while he perfected his artisan hybrid.

In 2006, Roelli released his first Dunbarton. While the taste sometimes seems a little more cheddar than blue and other times vice versa, the cheesemaking method is an even mix of technical styles. He adds classic blue molds (along with "secret cultures" he can't reveal) to the milk, and keeps the curds large, as is typical with blues so that air can circulate and react with the blue mold when he pierces the wheels during aging. He also "cheddars" the curds to get a little of that classic tang, yet packs the curd loosely as is done with blues. Before he sends the wheels to the cheese caves for piercing, Roelli prepares them by passing them through three different temperature-controlled environments (the specifics of which are also secret, he tells me, smiling sweetly) as part of his affinage treatment.

"I also got really lucky that the stuff I tried early on worked," he says, "because affinage likes to throw you a curveball."

Roelli typically ages Dunbarton for a little over two months. At this point it's a booze-pairing no-brainer. It likes big and fruity reds, but wouldn't discriminate against a mellow Carneros Pinot Noir either. As it gets older, it likes a little more sugar in its life and likes a nut brown ale or a Belgian tripel.

Westfield Farm Hubbardston Blue, Massachusetts

If Dunbarton Blue is a lovable yet rare blue-cheddar cheese unicorn, quick to please everyone from cheese novices who can't get enough of its soft cheddary goodness to caseophiles who marvel at its innovative sophistication, Hubbardston Blue is like a geodesic dome of cheeses. Some are amazed by its exquisite architecture and expert blending of functionality and form. Others are turned off by its complete unwillingness to conform to any blue stereotypes and that, well, especially earthy flavor it exudes.

Hubbardston Blue —

Hubbardston Blue from Hubbardston, Massachusetts, is a renegade goat cheese. Current cheesemaker Bob Stetson and his wife and co-owner, Debbie Stetson, who left their shipping business in 1996 to buy Westfield Farm after seeing an ad in the *Boston Globe*, says the main reason that the former owners Letty and Bob Kilmoyer decided to make Hubbardston Blue was because a big-time cheesemaker at the time told them it was impossible.

"Bob, if nothing else, was a contrarian," says the current Bob. "He was interested and fascinated by the process and needed to use that extra milk, but being told he couldn't was enough motivation." And so a weird and delicious cheese was created.

Hubbardston Blue is five ounces and looks like a cross between a Loire Valley ashed-style cheese and a bloomy-rinded cutie such as Scholten Weybridge. It's shaped like a hockey puck. Its surface is covered with a gray mold that looks like ash but is actually just blue mold gone powdery.

Inside, the cheese surprises. It looks like it's going to taste fresh and goaty like Selle sur Cher or Vermont Butter & Cheese's Coupoule and even has a thin layer of dark gray mold underneath the surface that looks like ash to add to the confusion, but instead it has the silky, smooth texture of many surface-ripened, bloomy-rinded cheeses, such as Kurtwood's Dinah (see page 62). But it doesn't taste like them. It tastes like a blue. Kind of. Well, it tastes like a blue cheese mixed with cream and earthy morel mushrooms that might still have a leaf or two attached.

The cheese's flavors can be partially explained by its production. When making Hubbardston, Stetson starts out with pasteurized milk, to which he adds cultures, that good ol' *Penicillium roqueforti* mold, and rennet. The rennet is vegetable, which can lend a cheese an earthy flavor right off the bat. After letting the mix sit for a couple hours, Stetson cuts the custard-like curd into ¾-inch pieces, drains off the whey as it develops, and ladles the curd into perforated cups to mold.

The next day he salts the cheese and puts it in a cabinet to dry. Five or six days later the cheese develops a bright blue, soft, powdery rind. At that point, the cheeses are wrapped in perforated paper. In the next two to three weeks the cheese softens, and as Stetson puts it, the "blue mold eats the cheese" under the paper. During this time the rind changes from blue to gray; a soft, thin rind develops; and Hubbardston ages, softening from the inside out like a surface-ripened Camembert style.

Blue cheesemakers traditionally pierce their blue by this point, allowing the air into the interior of the cheese so that the *Penicillium roqueforti* can breathe and propagate, forming blue veins. Westfield never does this, and it's this missed step and the wrapping of the puck in perforated paper that develops the unusual texture and mush-roomy, earthy character instead of the common sharp blue bite. The thin, ashy, slightly bloomy rind that develops over the blue mold? That's a lucky coincidence—ambient *Penicillium* mold that just happens to be kicking it in the aging room. Stetson doesn't add any other molds to the mix besides the *P. roqueforti*.

Stetson enjoys people's reactions when they taste his products. Unlike his other cheeses, Hubbardston elicits especially strong responses from those willing to try the unique creation (some are too scared).

"Some absolutely love the first bite," says Stetson, "others not so much. It's not like my other cheeses. If they like Hubbardston Blue, they adore it, and they are really disappointed if they come to the market and can't find it."

Because the flavors are so salient in the cheese, it's best to go with alcohol that has plenty of residual sugar left to buffer Hubbardon's firm edges. Sweet Rieslings, Gewürztraminers, and Chenin Blancs all work, as would a light dessert wine from, say, Southwestern France. Belgian tripels work well, too, and light-bodied pear liqueurs.

Westfield has another cheese to try that might please those with subtler tastes—still Hubbardston, but made with cow's milk. It's a bit gentler. There aren't many cheeses around exactly like this one to try, but there are many interesting blues and goat's milk blues fit for sampling if Hubbardston isn't near you: Rouge et Noir in Marin, California, makes Marin Chèvre Blue—a pierced, soft, bloomy-rinded disk that resembles Hubbardston slightly. Westfield makes a goat's milk, blue cheese–chèvre hybrid called Classic Blue Log. Caromont Farm in Esmont, Virginia, makes an ambient blue-ripened ashed goat called Alberene Ash (many are available by mail order, but are regionally focused. If pure goat blues are your game, Avalanche Cheese in Paonia, Colorado, makes one called Midnight Blue; Lively Run Goat Dairy in Interlaken, New York, makes Cayuga Blue; and Carr Valley in La Valle, Wisconsin, makes Billy Blue. Most can be mail-ordered and there are many more to be found locally.

Bayley Hazen Panna Cotta
with Rosewater Poached Pears

MAKES 6–7 SERVINGS

I had a goat cheese panna cotta years back that reminded me that cheese plus sugar plus cream equals deliciousness. While I was at a cheese shop trying to decide which chèvre to use to make my own version at home, blue cheese caught my eye. When it comes to rosewater pears, well, pears and blue cheese are a given, and rose confit or jelly and blue cheese are one of my favorite combos. With its buttery, sweet, caramel, lightly salty flavors, Bayley Hazen is a natural fit for this dessert. If substituting another blue, make sure to choose drier cheese such as Bohemian Blue or Point Reyes New Blue.

• Panna Cotta •

2 tablespoons water

7 grams powdered gelatin (one envelope)

2 cups half-and-half

⅓ cup and 2 tablespoons granulated sugar

½ vanilla bean

3 ounces Bayley Hazen Blue, without the rind, crumbled

¾ cup cream

Lightly grease the insides of six medium-sized ramekins with grapeseed, extra virgin olive, or coconut oil. Put the water in a small stainless steel bowl large enough to fit over the top of a saucepan later, and sprinkle the gelatin evenly over the water. Set aside to let bloom.

Place the half-and-half and sugar in a small saucepan.

Cut open the vanilla bean and scrape out the grains from the bean with the back of a paring knife into a small bowl. Add 2 tablespoons of the half-and-half mixture to the vanilla bean bowl. Stir with a fork or a small whisk to create a vanilla bean slurry.

Add the vanilla slurry to the pot and bring to 170 degrees on low to medium heat. At around 150 degrees, add the Bayley Hazen. Whisk well for 1–2 minutes to blend.

After the half-and-half mixture has reached 170 degrees, turn off the heat and use the pot as a bain-marie to liquefy the gelatin. Rest the gelatin bowl on top of the saucepan so the base of the bowl is resting an inch or more over the liquid. Stir the gelatin until it becomes a thick liquid. Set aside.

Pour the half-and-half mixture through a fine strainer into a large bowl. By this time, the mixture will have likely cooled to 130 degrees. If not, wait until it has reached 130 degrees. Once strained, add the gelatin, whisking vigorously until completely incorporated. Stir in the cream, mix well, and immediately pour into ramekins.

Put the ramekins on a sheet pan, cover lightly with foil, and refrigerate for 8 hours or overnight.

• Poached Pears •

2½ cups white wine
2½ cups water
¼ cup sugar
½ vanilla bean
zest of ½ a lemon
1 lemon, juiced
2 Bartlett pears
1 tablespoon rosewater

Bring the wine, ½ cup water, sugar, vanilla, zest, and half the lemon juice to a boil.

While the poaching liquid is coming to a boil, put the remaining water and lemon juice in a bowl. Peel, core, and cut the pears in half, and place immediately into the water lemon bath to prevent browning.

Once the poaching liquid is boiling, add the rosewater and bring to a low simmer. Add the pears and poach until a fork slides easily in and out of the fruit, in about 15 minutes. Once done, remove the pears and cool on a plate. Cover with plastic wrap and refrigerate until ready to use.

When ready to serve, cut around the inside edge of the panna cotta ramekin very gently with a thin paring knife. Place your palm on the top of the panna cotta and flip the ramekin over so your palm serves as a base. Slide the panna cotta onto your hand, then onto an individual dessert plate. Slice the pears into six slices per half and fan out the slices onto six plates.

Gouda Style and Inspirations

· · · · ·

Sweeter with Time

Americans couldn't be any more hooked on Gouda or its manifestations than if it were a hot dog or a peanut butter sandwich. Its sweet butterscotch or beefy flavors, its sometimes crunchy bite, its rich, firm texture. It's well known in the cheese business that if you run out of this top seller at a shop, you risk being shut down by its fanatic cult following.

There's not a lot of historical evidence of Dutch immigrants working much cheese influence in this country, so how Gouda became such a popular cheese in the United States, I'm not exactly sure.

But I do know that my own attachment to Gouda was formed when someone introduced my ten-year-old self to it. Besides "Brie," it was the first foreign cheese I'd ever had. It was European, and it made my permed, Keds-wearing self feel sophisticated. Maybe other American attachments developed in the same way as mine and people held on to those familiar memories. Or maybe it's that Gouda's sweet, caramelized flavors appeal heavily to the sugar-loving American palate. Or perhaps it's the Gouda crunch that comes from amino acid crystals that keep them coming back.

Whatever it is, Gouda, or the cheese style inspired by Gouda, Holland, is a mainstay in the United States. Actual "Gouda Holland"—a name protected by the European Commission—is made only in the southern town of Gouda in Holland, but the cheese has had such an influence here that when people make or taste wheels that are semi-hard to hard, mellow, and slightly sweet, they often call them Gouda. While it's a term of respect to some, this fact can irk cheesemakers (including one whose cheese I've included in this section) because, well, many cheeses could be described with those adjectives, some of which are even made thousands of miles away from Holland in the Pyrenees foothills. It can quickly become a blanket term.

Regardless of the misnaming, it's impossible to deny Gouda's influence. Whether or not someone calls their cheese by this name, Gouda's methods have made their mark here. There are cheesemaking techniques that, when combined, create a cheese whose tastes reflects that regional cheese. They are: using certain starter cultures; "washing the curds" (or delactosing); slowly cooking the curds; and pressing the curd under warm whey. These techniques are explored through the lenses of the cheeses in this chapter.

Branched Oak Nettle Gouda, Nebraska

It all started when their meat CSA customers began asking for milk. In six years, Doug and Krista Dittman at Branched Oak in Raymond, Nebraska, went from being a pasture-grazed beef and free-range chicken producer to becoming a full-fledged organic grass-fed creamery. The cows they originally bought to satisfy milk demand became the foundation of a small farmstead dairy, and the family left their meat business to build a creamery and set up permanent cheese camp.

One of the most moving of Branched Oak Farm's many cheeses is their seasonal Nettle Gouda. It is made when the year's first buds start to blossom. It is a nod to the traditional practice in Holland when many *Boerenkaas* farmstead, pasture-based Gouda cheesemakers celebrate the oncoming spring and new growth in the field by making cheese flecked with seasonal nettles growing in the meadow.

Semifirm and rich, Branched Oak's Nettle Gouda has buttery yellow paste provided from the milk of Jersey cows munching on the Dittman's Nebraska plain grasses. Embedded in the paste are thin, dried slices of dark green nettles.

If you haven't tasted nettles before, think slightly herbal. They're a little oniony like chives, but with less of a bite, a light lemon flavor, and more savory depth. Otherwise known as "stinging" nettles, this herb causes a stinging sensation on one's skin when brushed up against. Drying or a quick blanching in boiling water removes the histamines that cause the sensation. Cheesemaker Krista Dittman (her husband, Doug, is the cowman) uses the dried nettle form and then boils it once more to resanitize it, so when the herb goes in the cheese, it's as harmless as a sleeping baby.

Cheesemaker Dittman uses raw milk from their own herd for this Gouda. A bit unusual still in the creamery world, Krista and Doug milk their animals only once a day (most creameries, especially those with cows with high milk producers such as Holsteins, milk their animals twice a day to further production). It affords their Jerseys and their family a slightly more relaxed lifestyle.

That morning milk goes straight to the make room. It is heated to eighty-seven degrees, and then nettles, cultures, and rennet are added. The curds are cut, stirred, and then around 45 percent of the whey is poured off to make room for the classic Gouda hot water wash. Hot water is added to the curds, and the mix is stirred again for around forty-five minutes. Next, the curds are gathered and pressed under their own whey and the warm water, as is typical with many Goudas and Alpine-inspired cheeses to meld the curds and control acidity. Once matted, the "big body of curd," says Dittman, is pressed into hoops or molds then pressed in a machine for two hours to release whey. The next day they're brined. Then they're sent to the cellar for a year, and enthusiastic customers must sit on their cheese fingers until the wheels are ready for release.

For Krista, part of the cheesemaking draw from moving from meat to cheese was that cheese gave the family the ability to work with a product whose value would increase as it aged. Such is not the case with meat animals. But milk morphs and gains more monetary and social value when it is turned into cheese. You can charge more, and people often think of its second incarnation in higher regard. Says Dittman, "The value in agriculture is not just economic. Adding value in a sustainable system is adding social and environmental value, too. These things are harder to measure than economic, but there's big compensation."

It also helps that every day is different with cheesemaking. "I hate repetition," says Dittman. "I'd make a pretty lousy factory worker." One day you might be making quark, the next day Gouda, the next day you might be working at a farmer's market, or back at the farm trying to figure out how to alter your make to compensate for higher fat content in the milk.

Because this cheese is rich and full-bodied, pair with wines accordingly. Stick with simple, lightly oaked whites that match the creamy nuttiness in the cheese, such as Viogniers and Chardonnays, richer reds such as Syrahs and Zinfandels, and heavier beers. Bonus for those cheese lovers heavily into the pairing portion of cheese write-ups: Nettles are great for digestion and are a natural liver cleanser. Eat up.

If you can't find this small production cheese near you, there many other grass-based Goudas around the country, such as Burroughs Family Benina Crema from Oakdale, California; and Hidden Hills Dairy Old Gold from Everett, Pennsylvania.

Holland's Family Cheese Marieke Gouda, Wisconsin

Before Holland's Family Cheese opened in 2007 in Thorp, Wisconsin, finding a walnut-hued American Gouda with tiny crystals that crunch like hard candy was as difficult as hunting down Fruit of the Loom briefs in Neiman Marcus. Although big companies were wrapping mediocre cheese flavored with artificial smoke in red plastic and a few small producers were making excellent Gouda-inspired cheese, authentic versions of *boerenkaas* (farmhouse) Goudas in the United States weren't readily available. Cheesemaker Marieke Penterman made her mark.

Holland's Family Cheese Marieke Gouda is a Gouda lover's dream. Sturdy, firm, packed with that classic Gouda crunch that comes from calcium breaking down when aged over a year, Penterman's Marieke is as much an ode to Dutch cheesemaking traditions as Berkeley's Chez Panisse is an homage to French marketplace cooking.

Beyond all that seriousness, it just tastes like savory cheese candy, in a very good way. With pleasure comparable to biting into a salted caramel toffee or another sweet-salty/yin-yang favorite, in Marieke, butterscotch and crème de caramel meet robust beefy, salty flavors.

As it ages, its flavors intensify—it's an umami blitzkrieg. It's cheese, turned up to 11.

Made by Marieke Penterman, who started crafting her wheels after an inspirational dream and a desire to have the cheese of her Dutch childhood in the middle of Wisconsin, Holland's Family Cheese makes Goudas that could be mistaken for Dutch versions in a blind tasting. Nearly all Goudas get the heavy curd-washing and cooked curd treatment, but Penterman believes it's her strict allegiance to the Dutch methods and equipment that makes hers so different.

After completing the 240 hours of schooling and apprenticeship required of Wisconsin cheesemakers at the time, Penterman headed to Holland. She spent a couple days with *boerenkaas* producers—one who milked her ten cows by hand, and the other who had two hundred, and I hope had help to milk them.

There, she learned traditional methods, crafted her Marieke recipe based on what she thought were the best qualities of the two Dutch cheeses she witnessed being made, and brought home Dutch Gouda culture starters and pine boards on which to age her own wheels. She also arranged for a "Double O" or "8" cheese vat (shaped like an eight) to be sent from Holland.

The milk—all from her own cows, which is par for the course for Penterman, since she grew up with dairy farmers—sits for no more than five hours before it goes to the vat. There, it's slowly heated to under pasteurization and Penterman adds calcium (a typical Netherland and sometimes American practice), Dutch cultures, and rennet.

When the curds are very soft, she drains them and washes them by hand, turning them around in hot water until much of the lactic acid leeches off and the curds form into "little, soft pebbles." The cheese gets two pressings—one under whey—and is brined for two days. After putting them in an aging room to dry off, the wheels receive a poly coating—not wax, says Penterman, because only Goudas that were traditionally exported were waxed to help the cheese withstand the journey in the old days). Then, they're aged. Most for under twelve months, some for a year. I prefer the older.

From cow to wheel, Holland's Family Cheese nearly duplicates how Gouda is made in Holland. One difference (one that some think is a big one) between Penterman's version and *boerenkaas* is that her cows eat a diet of only dried grasses and hay. They aren't pastured, which all Dutch *boerenkaas* animals must be. After dealing with customers who didn't understand why the cheese tasted different per season, Penterman put her cows on a nonvariable diet to produce consistent milk.

She keeps her cows in freestyle barns where they have plenty of room to walk around, keeps fans on them, brushes them off daily, and politely insisted to this California native that they're happier than my state's cows, even those that munch on grass all day. "Cows don't like to sweat like they do in California," she explains.

After we chat a bit, we head to the cheese shop, where the youngest of her five children, four-year-old Fena, is helping to put price tags on the cheese for sale. She handles the price gun like a pro. My divination is that Holland's Family Cheese will have a long, fruitful life. When toasting to Marieke, eat this cheese with a malty ale, a Belgian double, or a rich California Pinot Noir.

Some other aged Goudas to try are Willamette Valley Cheese Aged Gouda from Salem, Oregon; and Winchester Cheese's Sharp and Super Aged Goudas from Winchester, California (both available regionally and through mail order).

Tumalo Farms Fenacho, Oregon

"Don't call it Gouda," said my tour guide at Tumalo Farms, cutting me off mid-sentence while we strolled across the gray desert gravel and sage brush to see the goats. "Or at least don't let Flavio hear you. Gouda's a place, he says, not a cheese," she said with raised eyebrow.

Cheesemaker Flavio DeCastilhos and his team craft cooked curd, pressed, and aged cheese such as Fenacho in the Oregon high desert that, to many, taste Gouda inspired. Americans accustomed to the artificially smoked cheese served with salami from their parents' picnic basket at Shakespeare in the Park labeled "Gouda" might not place it as such. But for the Americans who celebrate Gouda in all it's

⇨ Tumalo Farms Fenacho

artisan forms, Tumalo Farm's Fenacho seems related to the cheese named after the small North Holland town.

Coated in a light golden polyurethane film to preserve the rind, Tumalo Farm's Fenacho has a creamy white interior flecked with locally farmed fenugreek seeds—a classic flavor addition in Holland. The fenugreek adds a sweet butterscotch taste to the cheese's already floral, lemony base. Ask any of the Tumalo employees' children, who eat the cheese off the rind like a watermelon when not playing with the baby goats, and they'll tell you that Fenacho tastes a little like fresh and zesty, creamy cheese caramel.

Rather, it tastes like high-quality cream drizzled with a little goat caramel and studded with fenugreek. In Holland, adding seeds and spices to already exceptional milk is considered a fantastic way to add variety to the mix. Cheese snobs don't look down upon it as they do here, because there the flavorings aren't used to cover up mediocre milk, as is common with larger producers in the United States. In Holland, they often make two or three cheeses out of one already delicious, high-quality cheese base (bonus rounds).

Tumalo does it right, too. DeCastilhos started the farm in 2004 by selecting Saaman and French Alpine goats that like the climate in the 4,000-feet-above-sea-level Oregon desert near Bend. He lets them prance about on the fields and munch on desert brush here and there, but like Holland's Family Cheese, he doesn't let them graze for nourishment. Aiming for consistent-tasting milk, Tumalo feeds their seven hundred goats organic local alfalfa and grain to highlight the milk's fresh, naturally sweet flavors.

Even though Americans still think cow's milk for Gouda-style cheese, in Holland, they utilize both goat's and sheep's milk. No discrimination. Before he started Tumalo, former Silicon Valley professional DeCastilho's market research suggested that there was room for growth for aged sheep's and goat's milk from the United States (most were still from Europe when he started), and he was happy to fill the gap. When he went to Europe to visit cheesemakers and select equipment, he ended up staying longer in Holland because of his Van Gogh passion and had time to visit nearly a dozen cheesemakers and observe their process.

While DeCastilhos doesn't link his cheeses to Goudas in flavor—sometimes he denies any similarities at all—he does practice some methods typically utilized in Holland. However, as DeCastilhos points out, many of these techniques are also used to make Alpine or other mountain-style aged cheeses, too, and the combination of them doesn't make a cheese a Gouda. Which is true—Tumalo's other cheeses are also reminiscent of Abbaye de Belloc from the Pyrenees, for example. So time for full disclosure—I slipped Tumalo's Fenacho in this category because it makes me think of a cheese that's inspired by fenugreek-studded Gouda, not because Tumalo thinks or says it is.

As briefly mentioned when discussing Holland's Gouda in Wisconsin, one of the things that make Gouda-style cheese different from a cheese such as cheddar is what many Gouda producers call "washing the curds," and what DeCastilhos says is actually "delactosing." Before cooking the curds, hot water is added to the curds and whey. By applying heat, this cooks out some of the lactose and reduces the amount of milk sugar that the bacteria can turn into lactic acid later in the cheese's life. So the cheese ages better.

After delactosing, Fenacho curds are cooked on low heat for long periods of time. I thought this might increase the naturally sweet flavor in the milk as is done when onions are cooked on low heat for long periods of time and their sugars caramelize. DeCastilhos attests, however, that the flavor some (such as myself) perceive as "sweetness" in his cheeses is rather the freshness and quality of the milk showing up more as the cheese ages, the moisture leeches out, and the flavors concentrate the remaining flavors.

When pairing with Tumalo Farms Fenacho, I choose a wine that reflects the cheese's fenugreek butterscotch notes. That means going with an oaked white that is creamy and has hints of vanilla or wood from barrel aging. For whites I go with a soft, low-tannin variety such as Pinot Noir, Merlot, or Zinfandel, which won't overwhelm the fenugreek. Because of the distinct flavors in the cheese, it might also go with a subtle bourbon.

There are many American cheeses like Fenacho to try that have been influenced by methods utilized in Holland and elsewhere, or that align themselves to Dutch styles. Fenacho is widely available nationwide and via mail order, but some other good examples are La Clare's Evalon from Chilton, Wisconsin (goat's milk); Hillman Farm Harvest Goat Cheese from Colrain, Maine (available on the East Coast and a little beyond); and Keswick Creamery Vermeer from Newburg, Pennsylvania (cow's milk, also linked to Alpine styles, available mainly in Pennsylvania).

Marieke Gouda Almond Toffee

MAKES ABOUT 20 PIECES

With much inspiration from Tartine Bakery's toffee recipe, I created this dessert to highlight the butterscotch, nutty flavors in Marieke Gouda. Marieke traditional Gouda is terrific here, as are most semihard cow's milk or goat's milk Goudas. My favorite twist is to use a fenugreek-studded cheese such as Tumalo's Fenacho (which is not a Gouda, but still tastes good here). Read through the entire recipe before beginning, and have all your ingredients and equipment measured and ready to go when making this toffee because once it hits the proper temperature, you must move quickly or all will be lost (as I can attest). You will need a candy thermometer.

½ cup blanched, slivered almonds
3 ounces Marieke Gouda, without rind
1¾ cup granulated white sugar
½ cup salted butter
3 tablespoons water
1 tablespoon molasses
1 teaspoon vanilla
¼ teaspoon baking soda

Preheat oven to 300 degrees. Spread the almonds over a sheet pan and toast in the oven until they're evenly golden, about 5–10 minutes. Set aside to cool.

Cut the Gouda into small pieces about the size of pencil erasers or smaller.

Cut a piece of parchment paper large enough to fit the bottom of an 8- by 12-inch sheet pan (it should not cover the sides). Fit into the sheet pan. Use a tablespoon of butter to grease the parchment. Evenly distribute the Gouda over the sheet of parchment.

Put the sugar, butter, water, molasses, and vanilla in a

medium-sized, heavy-bottomed saucepan and heat over medium heat. Once the butter starts to melt, stir three or four times to combine. You want to stir the sugar mixture as little as possible. Once the butter is completely melted and all is combined, cook the mixture until it reaches 295 degrees on a candy thermometer, again stirring as little as possible. Then, add the baking soda and quickly stir to thoroughly combine. Immediately pour the hot toffee mixture evenly over the cheese. Use a greased cake spatula rubbed with butter to spread the mixture if needed. When cool enough to touch, pour almonds on top of the caramel and press down firmly so they stick to the top of the toffee.

Let cool for several hours, then break up with the tip of a paring or bird's beak knife to serve.

Acknowledgments

I would like to thank all the cheesemakers featured in the book for allotting me time for visits, interviews, and many follow-up questions. I'm so appreciative of your fitting me into your incredibly busy days.

I would also like to thank my recipe testers and tasters, and especially Sarah Johnson, Brandi Kozlowski, and Hannah Hoffman, who helped me refine my dessert recipes. Thanks also to Tia Keenan for recipe inspiration, to Molly DeCoudreaux, who photographed recipe sessions for my blog and beyond, and to Dianne Jacob, who taught the book proposal class that helped me realize I had a book inside me.

Thank you to the many people such as Paul Kindstedt, PhD, who were more than happy to spend time on the phone with me talking about American cheese history, and Heather Porter Engwall at the Wisconsin Milk Marketing Board, who helped with visits and beyond during my Midwestern cheese journeys.

Thank you also to my fabulous cohort at Solano Cellars and Vintage Berkeley; my friends and family for bearing with me and for your support; my terrific agent, Danielle Svetcov; my enthusiastic publicist, Heidi Richter; and to my book editor, Maria Gagliano—Maria, thank you for being a nice editor, and saying what the book needed in clear words. And thank you, Suzy Thompson, for your master indexing. To Daphne Zepos, thank you for living a life that will continue to inspire so many, and for giving us someone that we want to be when we grow up. My gratitude also goes to my blog readers; your comments have kept me going on more than one occasion.

References

Behr, Edward. "Pushing to a Delicate Extreme: The Cheeses of Soyoung Scanlan." *Art of Eating* 86 (2010), 5–13.

Caldwell, Gianaclis. *The Farmstead Creamery Advisor.* White River Junction, VT: Chelsea Green, 2010.

Dalby, Andrew. *Cheese: A Global History.* London: Reaktion Books, 2009.

Eekhof-Stork, Nancy. *The World Atlas of Cheese.* English version, edited by Adrian Bailey. New York: Paddington Press, 1976.

Estabrook, Barry. "A Tale of Two Dairies." *Gastronomica* 10.4 (2010), 48–52.

Janus, Edward. *Creating Dairying.* Madison, WI: Wisconsin Historical Society Press, 2011.

Kessler, Brad. *Goat Song: A Seasonal Life, a Short History of Herding, and the Art of Making Cheese.* New York: Scribner, 2009.

Kindstedt, Paul. *Cheese and Culture: A History of Cheese and Its Place in Western Civilization.* White River Junction, VT: Chelsea Green, 2012.

Kindstedt, Paul, with the Vermont Cheese Council. *American Farmstead Cheese: The Complete Guide to Making and Selling Artisan Cheeses.* White River Junction, VT: Chelsea Green, 2005.

McCalman. Max, and David Gibbons. *Mastering Cheese: Lessons for Connoisseurship from a Maître Fromager.* New York: Clarkson Potter, 2009.

Mendelson, Anne. "In Bacteria Land: The Battle Over Raw Milk," *Gastronomica* 11.1 (2011), 35–43.

Parr, Tami. *Artisan Cheese of the Pacific Northwest.* New York: Norton, 2009.

Paxson, Heather. "Cheese Cultures: Transforming American Tastes and Traditions," *Gastronomica* 10.4 (2010), 35–47.

Just Some of My Favorite Cheese Shops

CALIFORNIA

Bi-Rite
3639 18th Street, San Francisco, CA 94110
(415) 241-9760

Cheeseboard Collective
1504 Shattuck Avenue, Berkeley, CA 94709
(510) 549-9514

Cheese Plus
2001 Polk Street, San Francisco, CA 94109
(415) 921-2001

The Cheese Store of Beverly Hills
419 N. Beverly Drive, Beverly Hills, CA 90210
(310) 278-2855

The Cheese Store of Silverlake
3926 West Sunset Boulevard, Los Angeles, CA 90029
(323) 644-7511

Claremont Cave
325 North Yale Avenue, Claremont, CA 91711
(909) 625-7560

Corti Brothers
5810 Folsom Boulevard, Sacramento, CA 95819
(916) 736-3800

Cowgirl Creamery at the Ferry Plaza
1 Ferry Building, #17, San Francisco, CA 94111
(415) 362-9354

Cowgirl Creamery at Tamales Bay Foods
80 4th Street, Point Reyes Station, CA 94956
(415) 663-9335

Dedrick's Cheese
312 Main Street, Suite 105, Placerville, CA 95667
(530) 344-8282

Farmshop
225 26th Street, Santa Monica, CA 90402
(310) 566-2400

Mission Cheese
736 Valencia Street, San Francisco, CA 94117
(415) 484-6553

The Pasta Shop
1786 4th Street, Berkeley, CA 94710
(510) 250-6004

The Pasta Shop at Market Hall
5655 College Avenue, Oakland, CA 94618
(510) 250-6002

Rainbow Grocery Cooperative
1745 Folsom Street, San Francisco, CA 94103
(415) 863-0620

The Sacred Wheel
4935 Shattuck Avenue, Oakland, CA 94609
(510) 653-1353

ILLINOIS

Pastoral Artisan
2945 N. Broadway, Chicago, IL 60657
(773) 472-4781

MASSACHUSETTS

Formaggio Kitchen
244 Huron Avenue, Cambridge, MA 02138
(617) 354-4750

MICHIGAN

Zingerman's
610 Phoenix Drive, Ann Arbor, MI 48108
(888) 636-8162

MINNESOTA

France 44
4351 France Avenue South, Minneapolis, MN 55410
(612) 925-3252

Saint Paul Cheese Shop
1573 Grand Avenue, St. Paul, MN 55105
(651) 698-3391

NEW YORK

Bklyn Larder
228 Flatbush Avenue, Brooklyn, NY 11217
(718) 783-1250

Formaggio Essex
120 Essex Street, New York, NY 10002
(212) 982-8200

Lucy's Whey
425 West 15th Street, New York, NY 10011
(212) 463-9500

Murray's Cheese
254 Bleecker Street, New York, NY 10014
(212) 243-3289

Saxelby Cheese
120 Essex Street, New York, NY 10002
(212) 228-8204

Stinky Brooklyn
215 Smith Street, Brooklyn, NY 11231
(718) 596-2873

OKLAHOMA

Forward Foods
2001 W Main Street, Suite 111, Norman, OK 73069
(405) 321-1007

Forward Foods
5123 North Western Avenue, Oklahoma City, OK 73118
(405) 879-9937

OREGON

The Cheese Bar
6031 SE Belmont Street, Portland, OR 97215
(503) 222-6014

PENNSYLVANIA

Di Bruno Bros.
1730 Chestnut Street, Philadelphia, PA 19103
(215) 665-9220

TENNESSEE

The Bloomy Rind
501 Gallatin Avenue, Nashville, TN 37206
(615) 650-4440

TEXAS

Houston Dairymaids
2201 Airline Drive, Houston, TX 77009
(713) 880-4800

Scardello Cheese
3511 Oak Lawn Avenue, Dallas, TX 75219
(214) 219-1300

WASHINGTON

The Calf and Kid
1531 Melrose Avenue, Seattle, WA 98122
(206) 467-5447

WISCONSIN

Brick Street Market
104 East Walworth Avenue, Delavan, WI 53115
(262) 740-1880

Fromagination
12 South Carroll Street, Madison, WI 53703
(608) 255-2430

Larry's Market
8737 North Deerwood Drive, Milwaukee, WI 53209
(414) 355-9650

Nala Fromagerie
2633 Development Drive, Green Bay, WI 54311
(920) 347-0334

Schoolhouse Artisan Cheese
7813 Highway 42, Egg Harbor, WI 54209
(920) 868-2400

Index

Mayor of Nye Beach (Rivers Edge Chèvre), 169–172
Mayor of Nye Beach Crisped Rice Treats, 175
Maytag Blue (Maytag Dairy Farms), 180
Meadow Creek Dairy (Galax, VA), 113, 172–174
Meadow Melody (Hidden Springs Creamery), 69–71
Mélange (Andante Dairy), 76
Melon de Bourgogne, 19, 48, 147, 172
Mencia, 82
Mendez, Arturo, 29–30
Merlot, 126, 201
Mexico, influence on cheesemaking in the United States, 14, 21, 29, 34–36, 80–81
Midnight Blue (Avalanche Cheese), 187
Millan, Rico, 22
Miller, Angela, 93–94
Mimolette, 154, 160, 161
mixed milk cheeses, 67–76
   Benedictine, 71
   Buttercup, 71
   Crémont, 76
   Délice de la Vallée, 71–73
   Kunik, 73–76
   Meadow Melody, 69–71
   Mélange, 76
   Mona, 71
   Nancy's Camembert, 76
   Perlitta, 154, 159–162, 163–164
Mona (Wisconsin Sheep Dairy), 71
Monks, 14, 166
Mont St. Francis (Capriole), 172
Monterey Jack, 21, 42, 92
Moonflower (Garden Variety Cheese), 136
Moonshine (Bonnyclabber Country Cheese), 85–88
moonshine, for pairing with cheese, 80–82
Morford, Astraea, 170–171
Morford, Patricia, 170–171
Moscato D'Asti, 73
Mossend Blue (Bonnieview Farm), 181
Mouvedre, 107
Mozzarella, 2, 13, 14, 15–17, 18
   Lioni, 15–17
Mozzarella Company (Dallas, TX), 10, 31, 80–82
Mt. Tam (Cowgirl Creamery), 44, 56, 58, 62
mucor mold, 144
Muscadet, 19, 45, 147, 172
Mystery Bay Chèvre (Mystery Bay Farm), 2–4
Mystery Bay Farm (Nordland, WA), 2–4

Nancy's Camembert (Old Chatham Sheepherding Company), 64, 76
Narragansett Creamery (Providence, RI), 28–30, 38
Nathan Arnold, 110–113
Nebbiolo, 59, 145, 150
Nettle Gouda (Branched Oak Farm), 192–195
Nettle Meadow Farm (Warrensburg, NY), 62, 73–75
Nicasio Square (Nicasio Valley Cheese Company), 174
Nicasio Valley Cheese Company (Nicasio, CA), 59, 94, 174
Nielsen, Janice, 148–150

O'Banon (Capriole), 82
Ochoa Cotija, 34–36
Ochoa, Francisco, 34–36
Ochoa, Froylan, 34–35
Ocooch Mountain (Hidden Springs Creamery), 70
Ohlsen-Read, Jodi, 136–138
Old Chatham Sheepherding Company (Old Chatham, NY), 64, 76
Old Gold (Hidden Hills Dairy), 195
Old Kentucky Tomme (Capriole), 113
Olson, Myron, 95–97, 166
Oma (Von Trapp Farmstead), 167–169
Ossau Iraty, 134

Pacheco, Daniel, 158–159
Pacheco, Donna, 158–159
Pacheco, William, 158–159
paneer, 27, 28, 151
panela, 27
Parmigiano-Reggiano, 35, 149, 154, 155, 156
Pasta Filata, 13–25
pasteurization, xii, 35, 50, 86, 109, 137
Patenaude, Dan, 108
Patenaude, Jeanne, 108
Paula Lambert, 80–82
Pawlet (Consider Bardwell Farm), 91, 92–94
pear brandy, 80, 83, 84
pecorino, xii, 106, 130, 131, 132, 133, 135
Pecorino, Black Sheep Creamery's, 133
Pedrozo Dairy (Orland, CA), 110
Peluso, Franklin, 8–9
Penicillium candidum, 50, 56, 58, 61, 63, 74
Penicillium roqueforti, 83, 179, 180, 182, 185, 186
Penterman, Marieke, 195–197
Pepato (Bellwether Farms), 131, 133

Tomme de Savoie, 141
Tomme Delay (Lazy Lady Farm), 145
Trebbiano, 8, 9, 147
triple crème, 56, 60, 72, 73, 75
Tumalo Farms (Bend, OR), 198–201, 202
Twig Farm (West Cornwall, VT), 142–145
Txiki (Barinaga Ranch), 134–136

University of Utah, 125
Uplands Cheese Company (Dodgeville, WI),
    107–110

Valdéon, 83
Valencay (Lazy Lady Farm), 46
Valley Shepherd Creamery (Long Valley, NJ),
    154, 159–162
Valsetz (Rivers Edge Chèvre), 48
Van Laanen, Rachael, 3–4
Veldhuizen Family Farm (Dublin, TX), 107
Vella Cheese Company (Sonoma, CA), 153,
    154–156, 158
Vella Dry Jack (Vella Cheese Company),
    154–156
Vella, Ig, 85, 155
Vella, Tom, 85, 156
Verdejo, 34, 145, 150
Verdicchio, 19, 71
Vermeer (Keswick Creamery), 201
Vermentino, 19
Vermont Brebis (Willow Hill Farm), 136
Vermont Butter and Cheese Creamery
    (Websterville, VT), 42, 45–48, 62, 73,
    76, 185
Vermont Institute for Artisan Cheese, 122
Vermont Shepherd (Putney, VT), 129, 136
Viognier, 17, 76, 97, 120, 139, 145, 194
Vito Girardi, 18
vodka, 172
Von Trapp Farmstead (Stowe, VT), 167–169
Von Trapp, Dan, 167
Von Trapp, Sebastian, 167–169

Wabash Cannonball (Capriole), 42, 43–45
Wagon Wheel (Cowgirl Creamery), 94

Wajswol, Debra, 160–162
Wajswol, Eran, 160–162
Wallaby (Kenswick Creamery), 100
Watermelon and Burrata Salad with
    Pomegranate Molasses Vinaigrette, 24
weather, affect on cheese curds, 50, 75
Wehner, Jessica, 60
Welsh, Tim, 125
Westfield Farm (Hubbardston, MA),
    183–186
Weybridge (Scholten Family Farm), xi, 57–59,
    65, 184
white wine. See specific varieties
Widmer's Brick (Widmer's Cheese
    Cellars), 92
Wilcox, Shereen, 31–34
Wilcox, Todd, 33
Willamette Valley Cheese (Salem, OR),
    197
Willamette Valley Cheese Aged Gouda
    (Willamette Valley Cheese), 197
Willow Hill Farm (Milton, VT), 136
Winchester Cheese (Winchester, CA), 197
Winchester Gouda, Sharp and Super Aged
    (Winchester Cheese), 197
Winnimere (Jasper Hill Farm), 103
Winter's Caerphilly (Winter's Cheese
    Company), 123
Wisconsin Milk Marketing Board, 70
Wisconsin Sheep Milk Dairy Co-op (River
    Falls, WI), 162
Wisonsin Sheep Dairy (Catawba, WI), 71
Wit beers, 64, 172
Womanchego (Cato Corner Farms), 138
women, and their role in American
    cheesemaking, xiii, 42
wrapping and larding, 120

Yescas, Carlos, 29

Zinfandel, 107, 110, 120, 126, 133, 150, 162,
    194, 201
Zweigelt, 148

About the Author

Photo by Molly DeCoudreaux, MollyDecoudreaux.com

Kirstin Jackson is a cheese and wine writer and consultant, cook, and educator. Her work has appeared in the *Los Angeles Times*, the *San Francisco Chronicle*, NPR's *Kitchen Window*, *Kinfolk*, *Edible East Bay*, and on her blog, ItsNotYouItsBrie.com. Her classes at the Cheese School of San Francisco and 18 Reasons are regularly packed. Her cheese infatuation began early with dairy-inclined parents who drove her around Northern California on artisan cheese tours when she was a teenager, and her fascination with it only grew as she studied cultural anthropology and collaborated on regional food and wine oral histories at UC Berkeley. She lives in Oakland, California, and travels domestically and internationally to meet her dairy and wine needs.